THE
GOSPEL
FOR LIFE

—— SERIES ——

THE GOSPEL &

Work

Also in the *Gospel for Life* series

THE
GOSPEL
FOR LIFE

—— SERIES ——

THE GOSPEL &

Work

SERIES EDITORS

RUSSELL MOORE *and*
ANDREW T. WALKER

PUBLISHING GROUP

NASHVILLE, TENNESSEE

978-1-4336-9048-8

Published by B&H Publishing Group
Nashville, Tennessee

Dewey Decimal Classification: 174
Subject Heading: WORK \ BIBLE. N.T. GOSPELS \
WORK ETHIC

1 2 3 4 5 6 7 8 • 21 20 19 18 17

CONTENTS

Series Preface

Russell Moore

Why Should the *Gospel for Life* Series Matter to Churches?

IN ACTS CHAPTER 2, WE READ ABOUT THE DAY OF PENTECOST, the day when the resurrected Lord Jesus sent the Holy Spirit from heaven onto His church. The Day of Pentecost was a spectacular day—there were manifestations of fire, languages being spoken by people who didn't know them, and thousands of unbelievers coming to faith in this recently resurrected Messiah. Reading this passage, we go from account to account of heavenly shock and awe, and yet the passage ends in an unexpectedly simple way: "And they devoted themselves to the apostles' teaching and the fellowship, to the breaking of bread and the prayers" (Acts 2:42 ESV).

I believe one thing the Holy Spirit wants us to understand from this is that these "ordinary" things are not less spectacular than what preceded them—in fact, they may be more so. The disciplines of discipleship, fellowship, community, and prayer are the signs that tell us the kingdom of Christ is here. That means that for Christians, the most crucial moments in our walk with Jesus Christ don't happen in the thrill of "spiritual highs." They happen in the common hum of everyday life in quiet, faithful obedience to Christ.

That's what the *Gospel for Life* series is about: taking the truths of Scripture, the story of our redemption and adoption by a risen Lord Jesus, and applying them to the questions and situations that we all face in the ordinary course of life.

Our hope is that churches will not merely find these books interesting, but also helpful. The *Gospel for Life* series is meant to assist pastors and church leaders to answer urgent questions that people are asking, questions that the church isn't always immediately ready to answer. Whether in a counseling session or alongside a sermon series, these books are intended to come alongside church leaders in discipling members to see their lives with a Kingdom mentality.

Believers don't live the Christian life in isolation but rather as part of a gospel community, the church. That's why we have structured the *Gospel for Life* series to be easily utilized in anything from a small group study context to a new member or new believer class. None of us can live worthy of the gospel by ourselves, and thankfully, none have to.

Why are we so preoccupied with the idea of living life by and through the gospel? The answer is actually quite simple: because the gospel changes everything. The gospel isn't a mere theological system or a political idea, though it shapes both our theology and our politics. The gospel is the Good News that there is a Kingdom far above and beyond the borders of this world, where death is dead and sin and sorrow cease. The gospel is about how God brings this Kingdom to us by reconciling us to Himself through Christ.

That means two things. First, it means the gospel fulfills the hopes that our idols have promised and betrayed. The Scripture says that all God's promises are yes in Jesus (2 Cor. 1:20). As sinful human beings, we all tend to think what we really want is freedom from authority, inheritance without obedience like the prodigal son. But what Jesus offers is the authority we were designed to live under, an inheritance we by no means deserve to share, and the freedom that truly satisfies our souls.

Second, this means that the gospel isn't just the start of the Christian life but rather the vehicle that carries it along. The gospel is about the daily reality of living as an adopted child of a resurrected Father-King, whose Kingdom is here and is still coming. By looking at our jobs, our marriages, our families, our government, and the entire universe through a gospel lens, we live differently. We will work and marry and vote with a Kingdom mind-set, one that prioritizes the permanent things of

Christ above the fleeting pleasures of sin and the vaporous things of this world.

The *Gospel for Life* series is about helping Christians and churches navigate life in the Kingdom while we wait for the return of its King and its ultimate consummation. The stakes are high. To get the gospel wrong when it comes to marriage can lead to a generation's worth of confusion about what marriage even is. To get the gospel wrong on adoption can leave millions of "unwanted" children at the mercy of ruthless sex traffickers and callous abusers. There's no safe space in the universe where getting the gospel wrong will be merely an academic blunder. That's why these books exist—to help you and your church understand what the gospel is and what it means for life.

Theology doesn't just think; it walks, weeps, and bleeds. The *Gospel for Life* series is a resource intended to help Christians see their theology do just that. When you see all of life from the perspective of the Kingdom, everything changes. It's not just about miraculous moments or intense religious experiences. Our gospel is indeed miraculous, but as the disciples in Acts learned, it's also a gospel of the ordinary.

Introduction

Andrew T. Walker

"THE RAT RACE." "MY BOSS IS HORRIBLE." "I'M OVERWORKED and underpaid."

These are common phrases heard every day. There's no doubt that at some point, you have been irritated at your coworkers, your boss, or the daily routines that grow boring.

But did God design us to be miserable? To languish away in boredom?

No.

I recall being on vacation not long ago when a big Supreme Court announcement came down. I so badly wanted to drop what I was doing and pick up my computer so I could write and respond—so I could do my job. I didn't, because I needed to legitimately unplug from work.

But that caused me to reflect back and ask the question: Why would I choose to work over staring at the ocean for eight hours? Because God created every single person to work, contribute, provide, and thrive. It's in our bones. It's why people who are on vacation, though relaxed, grow miserable if their talents and skills aren't being tapped into. It's why someone who refuses to work isn't just being disobedient, but rejecting what it means to be human.

None of this should be a surprise to us.

The very beginning of the Bible is packed with God commissioning our ancestors, Adam and Eve, to take loving care and stewardship of creation. They were to work. They had responsibility tasks to tend to so that God's creation was being properly provided for. Work had to be done even before sin entered into the picture. Why?

God intends people to reflect the creativity of their Creator. We weren't made to be idle. Whether you have a blue-collar job or a white-collar job, the unique ways that God has gifted you and skilled you are meant to draw our wonder back to the Creator.

Work is something that everyone is going to do—has to do. That's why we decided to cover this understudied topic in the *Gospel for Life* series. We want to bring some of today's greatest Christian voices to bear on an issue that many people may not have thought about. The good news is that you don't have to hate your job, but with the right perspective, you can see what God is doing through you to take care of the family and communities around you.

Each book in the *Gospel for Life* series is structured the same: What are we for? What does the gospel say? How should the Christian live? How should the church engage? What does the culture say?

The Gospel & Work is intended to be an introductory look at how Christians should understand work and vocation from every angle of the Christian's life—their place in culture, their engagement as everyday Christians, and their role in the body of Christ, the church. We want no stone unturned when talking about how the gospel of Jesus Christ shapes us as a people on mission for God in every sphere of our life.

We hope that as you come away from this volume, you'll have a better understanding of what the Bible teaches about work. We hope that biblical principles shape our view of the nobility of work and that the vision we present is embraced. Work was ordained before the Fall. Thus, as image-bearers, we ought to labor for the glory of God, realizing that as we do, we reflect part of God's own nature. The theme of vocation pervades Scripture and must be understood from a biblical worldview. To this task we now turn.

What Are We For?

Bethany L. Jenkins

THE THING THAT THE LORD CARES MOST ABOUT IN OUR LIVES isn't who we marry or how many kids we have. It's not where we will live or what job we will take.

But it isn't that the Lord doesn't care about the details of our lives; He does (Matt. 6:25–34). It's just that the thing that He cares *most* about isn't our circumstances—it's our affections. He wants us to grow in our love for Him and others (Gal. 5:22–23). These other things—spouse, kids, home, and work—are good, but they are not ultimate.

Any conversation about faith and work, therefore, must begin here—with work in its proper place. Following Jesus out of darkness and into light, out of death and into life, is our ultimate calling. If we answer it, then we win at life (Col. 1:13; 1 Pet. 2:9; John 5:24; 1 John 3:14). If we don't, then we lose—no matter how successful we might be in our work.[1]

The Gospel Changes Everything

Once we *have* answered the call to follow Jesus, though, we must understand how this reality manifests itself in every aspect of our lives. For the gospel changes everything, including our work.

But what *is* the gospel?

The most popular presentation of the gospel in evangelical churches centers on Christ's life, death, and resurrection. It begins with our most fundamental reality—that we are sinners separated from God—and then offers the Good News that God, in His great love and mercy, is willing to forgive us through Jesus.

But this presentation of the gospel is incomplete. Amy Sherman explains:

> The glorious truths celebrated in this too-narrow
> gospel do not, in themselves, capture the full, grand,
> amazing scope of Jesus' redemptive work. For Jesus
> came preaching not just the gospel of personal jus-
> tification but the gospel *of the kingdom.* . . . It is not
> just about our reconciliation to a holy God—though

that is the beautiful center of it. It is also about our reconciliation with one another and with the creation itself.[2]

Similarly, in its "Theological Vision of Ministry," The Gospel Coalition states,

> The good news of the Bible is not only individual forgiveness but the renewal of the whole creation. God put humanity in the garden to cultivate the material world for his own glory and for the flourishing of nature and the human community. The Spirit of God not only converts individuals (e.g., John 16:8) but also renews and cultivates the face of the earth (e.g., Gen. 1:2; Ps. 104:30).[3]

If we want to understand how the gospel changes everything, including our work, then we must grasp its comprehensive significance. To do that, let's look at the Bible's narrative arc—creation, fall, redemption, and restoration—to discover the proper place of our work in light of God's larger work of redemption.

Creation

The first thing we need to know about work is that it is not a result of the Fall. Work is good. God made us to work. Part of what it means to be made in His image includes working and cultivating His creation (Exod. 35:31; Prov. 22:29):

> "Let us make man according to our image, after our
> likeness. . . ." And God said to them, "Be fruitful,
> multiply, fill the earth, and subdue it. Rule the fish of
> the sea, the birds of the sky, and every creature that
> crawls on the earth." (Gen. 1:26, 28)

He gave us dominion—that is, creative stewardship—over His creation. It is creative because we use the raw materials of His creation to build new things, and it is stewardship because, although God has given us authority to cultivate the world, He retains ownership of it. In this way, we are "sub-creators," as J. R. R. Tolkien puts it, working under God's sovereignty and delight as a form of worship.[4]

In Genesis 2, we see this kind of creative stewardship when God brings the animals before Adam to name them:

> The LORD God formed out of the ground every wild
> animal and every bird of the sky, and brought each
> to the man to see what he would call it. And what-
> ever the man called a living creature, that was its
> name. (v. 19)

Here, Adam is not sovereign over creation; God is. Yet God gives Adam authority to name His creation. Today, in the same way, we work as creative stewards when, for example, scientists name newly discovered elements on the periodic table or farmers till the ground to produce wheat for bread. They do not create *ex nihilo*—that is, out of nothing—like God does, but they steward His creation to bring forth good things.

The Fall

As a result of the Fall, though, our work is now marred with sin so that it is filled with "thorns and thistles" (Gen. 3:18). First, our relationship to work itself is distorted. Instead of seeing work as worship, we see it as a means of self-fulfillment and self-actualization, a way to "make a name for ourselves" (Gen. 11:4). Our willingness and ability to work for God's glory is tainted with pride, selfishness, and all kinds of sinful brokenness. We think of ourselves as entitled owners, not creative stewards.

Our working relationships with others are affected, too. Instead of serving one another in joy, we compete with one another in jealousy. We envy the success of others, thinking we deserve the promotions they receive. We tell white lies to our managers when telling the truth is risky. Like Adam, who said, "Don't blame me; blame the woman," and Eve, who said, "Don't blame me; blame the serpent," we shift culpability away from ourselves, taking credit when sales are up and listing excuses when they're down (Gen. 3:12–13, author's paraphrase).

Redemption

In Christ, though, God has begun His work of redemption in the world and in our hearts. He redeems our relationship with work because He becomes the center of our affections. When our identity is in Christ, not work, then success does not go to our heads, and failure does not go to our hearts. As Tim Keller says, "Faith gives us 'an inner ballast' without which work could destroy us."[6]

Christ redeems our relationships with others, too. When He subdued His enemies and died the death that we deserved, saying, "Don't blame them; blame Me," He unfurled His resurrection power to "restore all the ruins of the fall."[5] And this Good News becomes increasingly precious to us. We no longer need to envy the success of others because we can trust that God gives us all that we need (Ps. 84:11; Rom. 8:32). We can seek integrity and honesty—in big and small decisions—because we do not fear the opinion of others (Matt. 10:28; Ps. 20:7). By His Spirit we now have the power to turn work from a means of personal advancement to a vocational calling that is driven by selflessness, service, and love.

Restoration

And our present work ultimately points to our future destiny, the time when all things will be restored (Acts 3:21). At that time, though, we will not enter a garden, as in the original creation, but a city. Andy Crouch explains why this matters:

> Revelation 21:1 is the last thing a careful reader of
> Genesis 1–11 would expect: in the remade world, the

center of God's creative delight is not a garden but a city. And a city is, almost by definition, a place where culture reaches critical mass—a place where culture eclipses the natural world as the most important feature we must make something of.[7]

In other words, the main difference between creation and restoration is an abundance of culture—that is, human innovation and work applied to the raw materials of God's creation. It is apple pies, not just apples. It is structured companies, not just people sitting around tables. It is language, not just guttural sounds and grunts.

Anticipating this future reality shapes how we work today because it gives us hope that our work will one day be fulfilled. As Tim Keller observes, "If you're a city planner, there is a New Jerusalem. If you're a lawyer, there will be a time of perfect righteousness and justice."[8]

Yet our work in the here and now is only approximate—that is, a close but not exact—reality. When we work to glorify God and love others, we are sub-creators with Him, anticipating the restoration, but we recognize that the ultimate restoration of all things awaits the personal and bodily return of the Lord Jesus Christ (2 Pet. 3:13).

Our Vocational Assignments

The more we understand how the gospel redeems our work, the more we understand that our talents and gifts are not ours to keep, but to give away. They are not meant to be used for our own selfish gain, but for the glory of God and the good of others.

Paul says that God gives us "spiritual gifts" to do ministry and build up the church (1 Cor. 12). In accordance with these gifts, he says, each of us has a different role or assignment within the church:

> A manifestation of the Spirit is given to each person
> for the common good: to one is given a message of
> wisdom through the Spirit, to another, a message of
> knowledge by the same Spirit, to another, faith by
> the same Spirit, to another, gifts of healing by the
> one Spirit. . . . One and the same Spirit is active in all
> these, distributing to each person as he wills. (1 Cor.
> 12:7–9, 11)

Elsewhere, however, Paul does not limit the application of our gifts to church work only. In 1 Corinthians 7:17, he writes, "Let each one lead his life in the situation the Lord has assigned when God called him." Here, Tim Keller notes, Paul uses words like "calling" and "assignment," which he normally uses in the context of church work, to refer to work outside the church:

Paul is not referring in this case to church ministries, but to common social and economic tasks—"secular jobs," we might say—and naming them God's callings and assignments. The implication is clear: Just as God equips Christians for building up the Body of Christ, so he also equips all people with talents and gifts for various kinds of work, for the purpose of building up the human community.[9]

Our work is a vocational assignment, then, if God calls us to do it and if we do it for the sake of others, not ourselves. This is why some people refer to their work as their "vocation," implying that they don't just feel a strong sense of suitability for it, but that they sense that the Lord has assigned it to them.

This idea of vocational assignment, however, should not be over-spiritualized. As we have seen, our primary calling is to know Christ. Our vocational assignments are merely outgrowths of that calling, which means that knowing Christ is the everyday pursuit that fuels how we exercise our gifts and talents. When pastor Kevin DeYoung, for example, was at a career crossroads, his prayers focused less on his circumstances and more on his heart:

> I prayed a lot about the decision. But I didn't ask
> God to tell me what to do. So what did I pray for?
> I prayed that God would make me honest in my

interviews. I prayed that I would see a true picture
of this church and that they would see a true picture
of me. I prayed mostly that my heart would be right,
that I wouldn't be motivated by pride—either to
stay because it was a big church or to move because I
could be the senior pastor. . . . I prayed that I would
make a decision based on faith, hope, and love—
and not the praise of man and greed and selfish
ambition.[10]

This means that, when we are seeking our vocational assignment, we don't need to search anxiously for "Job Charming," as
my friend Dave Evans calls the mythical "perfect" job. Instead,
we can find a sense of purpose in every kind of work. As Paul
writes, "*Whatever* you do, do it from the heart, as something done
for the Lord and not for people" (Col. 3:23, emphasis added).

The Church Scattered and Gathered

Although we have each been given unique gifts and talents,
we exercise them in unison together. The Bible says that we are
"being built together for God's dwelling in the Spirit" (Eph.
2:22; cf. 1 Pet. 2:5). Yet we do this in two different ways—as
the church gathered and as the church scattered. When we
come together for corporate worship, we are "the church gathered." When we go out into the world to love and serve our

neighbors through our work in various places, we are "the church scattered."[11]

As the church scattered, we work in our vocations and fulfill the Great Commission. As Jesus told His disciples, "Go into all the world and preach the gospel to all creation" (Mark 16:15; cf. Matt. 28:19). Our workplaces are part of "the world," and "the whole creation" is everything from agriculture to business to government to art and more.

The public ministry of the church—from corporate worship to any other activity in which the church as an institution engages—is, therefore, distinct from individual Christians living out their everyday lives in the world. At the same time, though, individual Christians—though geographically separated—remain one body, working together to glorify God and contribute to the flourishing of their neighbors in their communities.

Pastors, then, should see their role not only as preaching the Word and administering the sacraments, but also as equipping the saints for service to the world during their workweeks. For the marketplace of the world, not the church, argues Abraham Kuyper, is "the race track where we wage the contest for the wreath." In a lecture to seminary students, he says,

> On behalf of the Lord Jesus Christ, Christians are
> engaged in a battle with the world. The gathered
> church is the heavenly, anticipatory eschatological
> army tent of the Lord and you pastors-in-training are

going to be field medics, strengthening the troops,
treating their wounds after battle, feeding them with
God's Word and sending them back out to take every
thought captive for Christ.[12]

We don't have to choose, therefore, between advancing the
local church as an institution and supporting the individual
Christians within that local church. It is a both-and, not an
either-or. Pastors can promote *both* "the primacy of word and
sacrament and the ultimacy of evangelism and discipleship in the
ministry of their church *and* the need for Christian worldview
thinking, vocation, cultural engagement, and more broadly, the
societal and cosmic implications of the gospel."[13]

The Masks of God

When we are the church scattered, we are "the masks of
God"—that is, His agents of His providential love. Luther notes
that God could have chosen to give us every good thing by
merely speaking a word or waving His hand, as He did in the
garden or in the desert. Instead, He chooses to use His image-
bearers to create and provide the things we need because He
wants us to be bound together in interdependent love, relationships, and communities.

For example, the psalmist praises God, saying, "He endows
your territory with prosperity; he satisfies you with the finest

wheat" (Ps. 147:14). But how does God do these things in practice? Luther writes:

> God could easily give you grain and fruit without
> your plowing and planting. But he does not want to
> do so. . . . What else is all our work to God—whether
> in the fields, in the garden, in the city, in the house,
> in war, or in government—but just such a child's
> performance, by which he wants to give his gifts in
> the field, at home, and everywhere else? These are
> the masks of God, behind which he wants to remain
> concealed and do all things. . . .
>
> Make the bars and gates, and let him fasten
> them. Labor, and let him give the fruits. Govern, and
> let him give his blessing. Fight, and let him give the
> victory. Preach, and let him win hearts. Take a hus-
> band or a wife, and let him produce the children. Eat
> and drink, and let him nourish and strengthen you.
> And so on. In all our doings, he is to work through
> us, and he alone shall have the glory from it.[14]

Elsewhere, when Luther teaches on the Lord's Prayer, he says that when we pray for "daily bread," we're praying for everything that must happen for us to have and enjoy it. He explains:

> You must open and expand your thinking, so that
> it reaches not only as far as the flour bin and baking

oven but also out over the broad fields, the farm-
lands, and the entire country that produces, pro-
cesses, and conveys to us our daily bread and all kinds
of nourishment.[15]

Amy Sherman offers helpful categories through which many
of us can view our work as masks of God.[16] In her list of God's
labors, she shows how we participate in His work:

- Redemptive work is God's "saving and reconciling
  actions." People who do this work include pastors, writers, counselors, songwriters, and more.
- Creative work is God's "fashioning of the physical and
  human world." People who do this work include paint-
  ers, seamstresses, carpenters, urban planners, and more.
- Providential work is God's "provision for and sustaining
  of humans and the creation." People who do this work
  include government workers, farmers, repairmen, bank-
  ers, and more.
- Justice work is God's "maintenance of justice." People
  who do this work include judges, paralegals, city managers, police officers, and more.
- Compassionate work is God's involvement in comfort-
  ing, healing, guiding, and shepherding." People who do
  this work are doctors, psychologists, nonprofit directors,
  welfare agents, and more.

- Revelatory work is God's "work to enlighten with truth." People who do this work are preachers, scientists, scholars, journalists, and more.

When we praise God for His protection and provision, for example, we recognize that people like police and farmers act as "the masks of God" to secure our borders and fill us with wheat. We celebrate that God is using His image-bearers to show us something of His goodness and to make us bound together in love. This also shows us that Christians can do almost any kind of work—from data-entry to education to medicine to so much more—as an offering of worship to God.

The Artificial Sacred-Secular Divide

Since all assignments are from God for the common good, then all work is "ministry" work. Martin Luther argued that all work done in faith is as much a vocational calling as the ministry of the monk or the priest. As The Gospel Coalition's "Theological Vision of Ministry" reads:

> Christians glorify God not only through the ministry of the Word, but also through their vocations of agriculture, art, business, government, scholarship—all for God's glory and the furtherance of the public good. . . . We have a vision for a church that equips

its people to think out the implications of the gospel on how we do carpentry, plumbing, data-entry, nursing, art, business, government, journalism, entertainment, and scholarship.[17]

In other words, some Christians are called to the pulpit, but others are called—in the same sense—to different vocations. The call to the pastorate, though important, is not "a higher call" than other calls; it's just a different call. The distinction between "sacred" and "secular" vocational callings is, then, artificial. As pastor Kevin DeYoung observes:

> Please don't ever think you are a second-class citizen in the kingdom of God if you aren't in full-time ministry. You can honor the Lord as a teacher, mother, doctor, lawyer, loan officer, or social worker; you can work in retail, fast food, politics, or big business; you can be a butcher, a baker, or a candlestick maker. You can be just about anything you want as long as you aren't lazy (Proverbs 6:6–11; 26:13–16), and whatever you do you perform to the glory of God (1 Corinthians 10:31).[18]

There are not, therefore, two worlds—sacred and secular—but one world that is created and fallen, that is being redeemed, and that will one day be restored. And Christ's lordship extends over every aspect of it. As Abraham Kuyper says, "If God is sovereign, then his lordship must extend over all of life, and it cannot be restricted to the walls of the church or within the Christian orbit."[19]

How Now Shall We Work?

In light of this high view of work, where there is no artificial sacred-secular divide, and where we work as creative stewards over God's creation awaiting the restoration of all things, how now shall we work? What do our workweeks look like? In its "Theological Vision of Ministry," The Gospel Coalition offers some ideas:

> Such a church [that integrates faith and work] will not only support Christians' engagement with culture, but will also help them work with distinctiveness, excellence, and accountability in their trades and professions. Developing humane yet creative and excellent business environments out of our understanding of the gospel is part of the work of bringing a measure of healing to God's creation in the power of the Spirit. Bringing Christian joy, hope, and truth to embodiment in the arts is also part of this work.[20]

Conceptually, it's helpful to look at three different lenses through which we approach work—heart, community, and world.

Heart

The gospel changes our heart motivations for work from selfish gain to worship and service. Instead of working to make a name for ourselves, we work to give glory to God and to serve others. Tim Keller observes that there are any number of potentially legitimate, biblical reasons that can motivate our work—from furthering social justice in the world to being personally honest and evangelizing our colleagues to creating beauty and wonder to working with a grateful, joyful, gospel-changed heart through all the ups and downs.[21]

The gospel also changes the honor we ascribe to work. When following Christ is our ultimate good, work can return to its proper place. On the one hand, we do not make it an idol and become workaholics because our loves are ordered with Christ at the center. On the other hand, we do not dismiss it and approach it with laziness because we know that our work is an assignment from God for His glory and the good of others.

Community

The gospel also changes how we relate to others. In our jobs, we are in relationships with many people. People in business are in relationship with their employees, their customers, and their suppliers. Lawyers are in relationship with their colleagues, their clients, the court and the judge, and more. Teachers are in relationship with their students, their students' parents, their principals, and more. The gospel changes all of these.

For example, if we are managers, the gospel changes how we lead at work. Katherine Leary Alsdorf says that, as she came to understand the gospel, "it was clear that, as a leader in the workplace, I can't be a model for goodness. Instead, I have to be the model of a repentant and redeemed sinner."[22] In other words, her testimony was not merely by sharing the gospel with words, but by exhibiting a lived-out repentant lifestyle. She didn't need to pretend like she was faultless; she just needed to show that, in her imperfections, she was humble.

World

Finally, the gospel also changes the world and the culture in which we operate—whether that is a particular firm or industry or the culture at large. Our work has ripple effects that reach far beyond what we can imagine at any given point in time. Small decisions at banks, for example, can impact an entire housing market. A new technological innovation can disrupt old systems. When these decisions and innovations are made for self-serving purposes, dangerous things can happen. When, however, they're intended for God's glory and the love of others, people can flourish.

The Role of Wisdom and Discernment

Finally, it's important to remember that we are like the exiles living in Babylon. As the scattered church, we live and work in environments that don't share all of our values. In fact, we're sometimes the only ones in our workplaces trying to do the right things, which means that we're often thinking through complex issues when things are unclear. The Bible doesn't offer a set of rules to obey, like whether to work for a cigarette company or whether to dismiss a particular employee. Wisdom requires going to God for discernment. The Holy Spirit is immensely powerful and omnipresent, so redemption is not ours to bear. But for our own joy and peace, it helps to build a relationship with God on a daily basis—not just in our moments of need.

After all, seeking His face is answering the ultimate call to know and follow Jesus and, if we do that, then we win at life and work.

Discussion Questions

1. How do you feel about your work? Has there been a time that it has been more or less meaningful?
2. In the category list of God's labors and our work, where does your vocation fit? How can this add meaning or shed light to your work?
3. How does your work give you a unique vantage point to see the brokenness of your heart (motivations), community (relationships), and world (industry)?
4. How does your work give you an opportunity to bring healing in each of those three areas?

What Does the Gospel Say?

Bruce Ashford and Benjamin T. Quinn

Yet it is too imprecise to say merely that Christian ethics "springs from" God's gift in Jesus Christ. What is the logic of this "springing"? What is it about God's gift that carries the promise of ethical illumination with it? We shall argue for the theological proposition that Christian ethics depends upon the resurrection of Jesus from the dead.[23] —Oliver O'Donovan, *Resurrection and Moral Order*

IN THE QUOTE ABOVE, OLIVER O'DONOVAN—ARGUABLY THE most significant evangelical ethicist of our day—notes the importance of grounding Christian ethics not merely in the "gift of Christ" but in the "resurrection of Jesus from the dead." Thus, for any discussion concerning the gospel and its relationship to Christian living, it is the resurrection of Christ that anchors the Christian's calling and initiates meaningful service in God's world. As 1 Corinthians 2 insists, "Christ and him crucified" changes nothing without "Christ, the resurrected Lord." It is precisely because of Christ's resurrection that the virgin birth, sinless life, and death on the cross enthrone the carpenter from Nazareth as the King of creation who *calls* His people to *walk in His way*.

But, what does it mean to *walk in the way of Christ*, and why does it matter for Christian vocation?

In Scripture, the *way* is a mega-metaphor signifying the fact that God's lordship should *shape* and *direct* the totality of Christian living. In Deuteronomy 10:12, Moses signals the importance of *way* for God's people when he summarizes God's ultimate expectations for them and includes "way" alongside other dominant biblical imperatives such as "fear the LORD" and love for God with all of one's "heart and all your soul." He writes, "And now, Israel, what does the LORD your God ask of you except to fear the LORD your God by walking in all his ways, to love him, and to worship the Lord your God with all your heart and all your soul?"

In other words, Moses appears to include walking "in [God's] ways" alongside the most important commandments in Scripture—including the Great Commandment. As the biblical story continues, *way* only increases in prominence. It is prominent in Psalm 1 and 119 and in Proverbs 1–9 (especially 4 and 9). It is found throughout the prophets who scold God's people for neglecting the "ways of the Lord." We see it employed in the Gospels when John the Baptist "prepares the way of the Lord," and Jesus declares that He is the "way" (John 14:6). It continues in Acts 9:2 when Christians are called people of the "Way," and when Paul urges Christians to "live worthy of the calling you have received" (Eph. 4:1).

In light of the prominence of "way" language in the Bible, it is not surprising that there is a strong link between the gospel and a Christian's way in this world. Because of the Lord's crucifixion and resurrection, we are now set free to bring all of life under submission to His lordship, to shape and direct all of our activities in light of His Word.

In the rest of this chapter, we will explore how this link between gospel and *way* relates to Christian vocation. We begin by defining gospel and vocation. From there, we consider how the Good News of the resurrected Christ forever changes our view of the created world and its cultural activities, and of creation's relationship to Christ. Finally, in light of this relationship, we will offer three demands that the gospel makes on vocation for Christians.

Defining the Gospel

The Christian gospel is a message of "good news." In His preaching ministry, Jesus gave some very special news about God's Kingdom. If this is true, then "gospel" or "good news" in the ancient world is best understood as a media term. It is a proclamation of a news event, a *good* news event.

The term is also used in other ancient material outside of the Bible. When "gospel" is used in the ancient world outside the confines of the biblical material, it is employed to describe the announcement of an important event. The word "gospel" describes, for example, the capture of a city, the defeat of an opposing army, the entrance of the king into a town, or a message about a king's activities.[24]

In Scripture, however, the gospel is not a message about the capture of a city or the defeat of an army. Particularly, in the New Testament, the gospel is a message about Jesus. There are two questions we must answer to make this message clear: *Who is Jesus according to the gospel?* and *What has He done?*

First Corinthians 15:3–5 is one of the most concise formulations of the gospel message in Scripture, and is a helpful way to quickly address who Jesus is and what He has done. Almost everyone agrees this passage is an early shorthand exposition of the gospel. John Dickson describes these verses as a "bullet point summary of the gospel."[25]

In these verses we find one of the earliest creeds of the Christian church. These verses carry the content of the very "gospel" that Paul preached to the Corinthians (according to 15:1) and it is "by this gospel" that the church is saved (15:2). It is this gospel that Paul himself received, and that he delivered to the church (15:3). So what does the apostle Paul say the gospel is? He says:

> For I passed on to you as most important what I also
> received: that Christ died for our sins according to
> the Scriptures, that he was buried, that he was raised
> on the third day according to the Scriptures, and that
> he appeared to Cephas, then to the Twelve. (1 Cor.
> 15:3–5)

According to Paul, the gospel is an announcement that he received and that he can also deliver. The "gospel" is a message about Jesus. The format of these verses indicates to us that the message Paul proclaims is a confession, a creed that is to be recited over and again. It is a confession about the person and work of Jesus. The specifics of the message are very, very important. The specific affirmations of the gospel are as follows:

1. The gospel identifies Jesus as Christ.
2. The gospel affirms that Jesus died a saving death.
3. The gospel affirms that Jesus died a saving death *for sin*.
4. The gospel teaches that Jesus died and was buried.
5. The gospel proclaims that Jesus was raised/resurrected.
6. The gospel says that Jesus' death and resurrection were in line with the Scriptures' teaching.
7. The gospel confirms that Jesus appeared to witnesses who saw His resurrected body.

In brief, Christ died and rose to deliver the world from sin, and He lives to bring the whole world under His authority as King. There are many ways of summarizing this gospel. Paul summarizes it nicely in 1 Corinthians 15:3–5, though he does so differently in passages such as Romans 1:3–4 and 2 Timothy 2:8.

For the purposes of this chapter, we summarize the gospel as *"the announcement that God's kingdom arrived in the life, death, and resurrection of Jesus, who is King and Savior, in fulfillment of Old Testament prophecy. The gospel calls for belief, trust, and repentance; to those who heed this call, he gives the privilege to live with him eternally in the new heavens and earth."* More succinctly, *"The gospel is the announcement that Jesus the King died and rose again in order to save us from our sins."*[26]

Defining Vocation

The English word *vocation* is derived from the Latin word *vocatio*, which means "calling." Christ calls us in general and specific ways. In the general sense, all who believe in Christ and are born again have, therefore, been called into the family of God to walk faithfully with Him forever. We believe that this call is for all people everywhere to believe in Jesus, though Scripture is clear that not everyone will hear and believe. Nevertheless, God in His grace has chosen to redeem a people for Himself who live as citizens of the heavenly Kingdom, loving God and loving others in this world until His Kingdom comes "on earth as it is in heaven."

In a more definite sense, God calls His people to play specific roles in His Kingdom. Although all Christians share the general calling to salvation, each of us has a specific role in the Kingdom, and our role will not be exactly the same as other Christians. Although all of us—together—are part of God's Kingdom, family, and body (important communal images from Scripture), each of us as individual citizens, siblings, and members need clarity about our particular role.

In this more specific sense, we define calling as *the way or ways we make ourselves useful to others.*[27] There are several things to consider about this definition, beginning with the language of "others." God did not create us to live for ourselves, but instead to live for others. The first "other" is God Himself. This is why the Great Commandment begins with the instructions, "love the LORD your God with all your heart, soul, mind, and strength." To begin with an "other" besides God would be idolatry. But, as Jesus taught, the second is like the first; we are to "love our neighbor as ourselves." "Self" simply serves as the pivot-point from which we direct our love and energy upward then outward.

Second, consider the language of way/ways. The first thing to notice is the plural, "ways." Despite the grammar, "vocation" is not singular. Often when we hear the word *vocation* we immediately think of our place of employment, and indeed this is *a* vocation. But, it isn't the only one. *Vocation* simply means "calling," and each of us inhabits multiple callings. For a Christian, the first calling is to Christ, Himself. Through our union with Him we live out other callings in the arenas of family, church community, neighborhood, and occupation or place of employment. There may be more vocations for some, but probably not less.

Work is an important handmaiden to vocation.[28] In fact, we view work as the *hand* that animates the *glove* of our vocations. Imagine a leather glove lying on your kitchen table. In order for it to be useful, you must slip your hand inside the glove. But, you can't simply shove your hand into the glove however you choose; you must slide each finger into the proper sleeve in order for the glove to be maximally useful, indeed useful at all.

We understand work and vocation to relate in similar fashion. We are *called* to multiple arenas in life and thus to occupy multiple vocations. The proper *way* to work out our vocations is by always striving for God-love and neighbor-love. But these vocations do not exercise love for God and His world until our fingers properly fill out the entire glove of our vocations and we get to work.

What the Gospel Declares about Our Resurrected Lord

Now that we have set forth our understanding of gospel and vocation, we must address how the two relate. In other words, what is so significant about the gospel that we should wonder how it affects our "9–5," and "5–9"? After all, doesn't "believing the gospel" pertain to one's current spiritual condition and eternal spiritual state? Indeed, it does, but that is only the beginning.

Because of the gospel—Jesus' victory over sin, death, and the grave, followed by His declaration of authority over all things (Matt. 28:18)—all of life, including our vocations, is laced with meaning and mission. His kingship over the whole of creation completely shapes how we understand our participation in the world—indeed, for our participation as citizens in His Kingdom.

Thus, we begin by recognizing that the gospel declares the Resurrected Lord as King over all time and space. Abraham

Kuyper famously declared, "There is not a square inch in the whole domain of our human existence over which Christ . . . does not cry, 'Mine!'"[29] We heartily affirm Christ's authority over every square inch. And, we offer this addendum that "there's not one single second on the whole of the worldwide calendar when Christ has not called a meeting," affirming His lordship over all *time* as well as *space*.

While few Christians have contested Christ's all-encompassing lordship historically, many Christians—especially in the West—have struggled to acknowledge His lordship outside the walls of church buildings (all spaces), and beyond dedicated worship times on Sundays (all times).

As such, Western Christianity, broadly speaking, has happily enthroned the Resurrected Lord as King over Sundays and church buildings. But we have tended to minimize His lordship over our Mondays through Saturdays, and our activities outside of the four walls of a church building. Certainly, we have acknowledged the Bible's straightforward commands about financial and sexual ethics. But beyond such straightforward commands, we have spent far too little time asking how God's saving works and Word should shape our activities in the arts and sciences, business and entrepreneurship, politics and economics, or sports and competition.

We tend to minimize His lordship in these ways because we have bought into the sub-biblical notion of a "sacred-secular" divide. While we believe most Christians have innocently ingested this dichotomy, it is antithetical to Jesus' declaration in Matthew 28:18 that "All authority has been given to me in heaven and on earth," and therefore this separation *must be consciously rejected*. In our view, it is precisely this kind of thinking that leads Christians to wonder if their work and vocations bear any real meaning and purpose.

Second, then, the gospel declares the Resurrected Lord as King over all of life. This first reaffirms Christ, the Creator, as the author of life from beginning to end. But now, in light of the Incarnation followed by the glorious Resurrection, the Son is not merely the *author of life*, but is the *defeater of death by death* whereby He has made it possible for the dead to be reborn. John Behr captures this well, arguing that "Christ has changed the 'use' of death for all men and women throughout time."[30] He further adds:

> This new "use of death" is not an act of desperation
> bringing about the end, or an act of passive sub-
> mission to victimization, resigning oneself to one's
> fate. It is, rather, the beginning of new life for the
> baptized and for those around them, a new mode
> of existence—"in Christ" rather than "in Adam"—
> manifest in the baptized. *Yet it is so only to the extent
> that they actively take up the cross, that is, no longer live*

> *for themselves in an ego-centric mode of life, but rather*
> *live ecstatically, beyond themselves, for their neighbors*
> *and for God.* "[31]

Behr's final sentence is especially important, as we shall see in the next section.

Third, the gospel declares the Resurrected Lord as Redeemer of all that is seen and unseen. Given the previous two, this point should go without saying. We find it important to reemphasize, however, because in the same way that Western Christianity has tended toward relegating Christ's lordship to Sundays and church buildings, it has also tended toward applying Christ's lordship only to the "spiritual" (unseen) part of creation, and neglecting the rest.

The Scriptures insist, however, that all of creation—heaven and earth, seen and unseen, "all things"—were made by, through, and for Christ. The Christ hymn of Colossians 1:16–20 famously celebrates this in the following words:

> For everything was created by him, in heaven and on
> earth, the visible and the invisible, whether thrones
> or dominions or rulers or authorities—all things
> have been created through him and for him. He is
> before all things, and by him all things hold together.
> He is also the head of the body, the church; he is
> the beginning, the firstborn from the dead, so that

he might come to have first place in everything. For
God was pleased to have all his fullness dwell in him,
and through him to reconcile everything to himself,
whether on earth or things in heaven, by making
peace through his blood, shed on the cross.

This perspective is by no means unique to Paul in Colossians.
Deuteronomy 10:12ff, discussed above, amidst the imperatives
to fear God, walk in His ways, love Him, and serve Him,
reminds the Israelites, "The heavens, indeed the highest heavens, belong to the LORD your God, as does the earth and everything in it" (v. 14). Psalm 24:1 echoes the same in its opening
verse, declaring, "The earth and everything in it, the world and
its inhabitants, belong to the LORD."

Thus, Paul's celebration of Christ as Creator and King joins
the canonical chorus that all is God's. Further, we conclude from
this that what God made good in Genesis 1–2, sin did not make
bad in Genesis 3. Though sin misdirected God's good world and
all that is in it away from Him to follow a different *way*, God
did not relinquish the rights to His world. Instead, He so loved
the world that He enacted a wise and sovereign plan to redeem
it. God sent Jesus, who is the Way, to prepare the way for all who
believe in Him to walk in His way forever.

What the Gospel Demands of
the Redeemed of the Lord

In this *way*, then, we—the redeemed of the Lord—must walk. This *way* shapes and directs every place and time in which we live, and it makes demands on our lives—beginning with the humble recognition that everything we have in life is a gift from God.

Paul asks the Corinthians in 1 Corinthians 4:7, "What do you have that you didn't receive? If, in fact, you did receive it, why do you boast as if you hadn't received it?" To begin with the confession that "all is gift" promotes a humble posture before God, and before our vocational tasks. This returns us to Genesis 1 to behold God as the great gift-giver. Everything that is both made and made possible by God is a gift given to those who bear His image.

Every time, place, possession, talent, relationship, and opportunity is a gift from the hand of God. Did we create our time? Our places? Did we endow ourselves with intelligence or talents with which we carry out our vocational responsibilities? No. All that we have—indeed, all that is—is given by the Creator and King. And, *our vocations serve to steward these gifts unto the King.*[32] As Alexander Schmemann urges in his excellent book *For the Life of the World*:

All that exists is God's gift to man, and it all exists to make God known to man, to make man's life communion with God. It is divine love made food, made life for man. God *blesses* everything He creates, and, in biblical language, this means that He makes all creation the sign and means of His presence and wisdom, love and revelation: "O taste and see that the Lord is good."[33]

A second demand that the gospel makes on our vocations is the love for God and neighbor in all times and places. God-love and neighbor-love cannot be overstated here as it characterizes both the *end* and *means* of walking in the *way* of the Lord. The humble confession that "all is gift" corresponds to the "fear of the LORD," which is the beginning of wisdom and the starting point for the *way* of the Lord (Prov. 1:7; 9:10). The first step down this *way* is a self-denying one that acknowledges and adores God as Creator, then proceeds in Christlike fashion emptying oneself (Phil. 2:7) in service to God and His world.

The degree to which we fashion our vocations around this cross-shaped *way* that loves God with all of our being, then loves others, is the degree to which our vocations matter in God's world. Thus, this double-love approach is the ultimate goal of every vocation, and the attitude with which we should carry out our responsibilities.

Jesus was clear that nothing is more important than loving God and neighbor (Mark 12:30–31). If this is true, then every vocation must consider the question: How does love for God and neighbor affect the *way* that I do my job? Whether business, politics, food service, secretarial support, education, coaching, construction, medicine, truck driving, parenting, and beyond, aligning our vocations with proper love for God and neighbor aligns the *way* of our vocations with the *way* of the Lord.

Let us not miss that this demand includes a genuine love for others. How can we carry out neighbor-love without loving and enjoying people? Perhaps the most common vocation-related complaint concerns interacting with people. How often have we heard, "If it weren't for 'so-and-so' I would love my job"? Moreover, how often have we said this ourselves? Here is a place where much reflection and repentance is needed. Across all vocations, may the redeemed of the Lord be known as those who love.

Third, the gospel demands that the redeemed of the Lord recognize their vocations as *ministry*. The Bible tells us that God often does His work for the world through the hands and feet of His people. He provided for the poor through the work of the entrepreneurial woman of Proverbs 31 and for the nation of Israel though Bezalel the artist. But how, practically speaking, does He provide for the world through ordinary jobs that most people have today?

When God feeds children, He usually does so through a vast and interconnected web of vocations. Before the farmer sows seed, the engineer has to design the tractor, and the mechanic has to assemble it. After the farmer gathers the crop, he depends upon the wholesaler to deliver the crops to the storeowner who sells to the young mother who feeds her hungry babies. The same thing goes for the way God often heals those who are sick, provides shelter for those who need a home, and offers enjoyment for those in need of recreation. Through *our* work, God conveys His love and provides for His world. What is this, if not *ministry*?

Moreover, when we consciously recognize our role as conduits of God's love and provision, our work takes on new dimensions. We begin to do our work with excellence, because if we are the "hands of God" through our job, we want those hands to provide the best service and the best product. We look forward to serving our coworkers and customers, because we realize that our interaction with them is in one way or another an extension of our Christianity. We look for opportunities to speak the gospel (words of life!) to those around us, as we realize we might be the only person they know who would speak the gospel to them.

Our workplace, then, is a place of bona fide *ministry*. We should approach it in this manner, confident that, at least for the time being, God has placed us in this particular job for reasons only He knows entirely. Even if we struggle to see how God is working through our work, we can be confident that He is.

Finally, the gospel demands that God's people are empowered by God's Spirit to redirect creation back to God. Faith in Christ gives us eyes to see and ears to hear God's world afresh. We not only see how things *are*, but how they *ought* to be. Take, for example, Paul's exhortation to the Thessalonians to work hard and avoid laziness and nosiness (2 Thess. 3:6–15). Paul calls the Christians in Thessalonica to recognize that the way some *are* working is not the way they *ought* to work. Instead, we must redirect the sin of sloth in order to "live quietly, and to mind [our] own affairs, and to work with [our] hands . . . so that [we] may *walk* properly before outsiders and be dependent on no one" (1 Thess. 4:11–12 ESV, emphasis added).

Illustrations are manifold here, but perhaps none is more vivid than the example of the artist. The artist *keeps* and *cultivates* beauty in God's world. For many, however, art is a means of perversion, promoting the worship of creation rather than the Creator. This devolves further when faux beauty mixes with commercialism and is distributed in mass, prostituting both the artist's ability and beauty, itself. The Spirit of God empowers God's people to see what *is* and what *ought* to be in the arts. When perverted art masquerades as "beauty," the Spirit-filled artist is able to reorder the perversion back toward God, promoting art that corresponds to beauty, itself.

Conclusion

The gospel of Christ declares Jesus as King over the whole of creation—all time and space, all physical and spiritual, all that is seen and unseen. By faith in this gospel, God's people join Him on His mission of making disciples of all nations and, ultimately, of making all things new. This is carried out most often in the ordinary, everyday vocations of God's people who walk in the *way of the Lord*. At work, at home, at the ball field, at church, and in their neighborhoods, God's people love Him with all of their being and love others as themselves. This *way* of life serves to spread the fragrance of Christ across His world as God's people speak and live the Good News of Jesus, the King, who bids us come and walk in His *way*, forever.

How certain can we be about this? We can be as certain as the resurrection of Christ that anchors and initiates meaningful service in God's world, then empowers us on the *way* that shapes and directs all of life.

Discussion Questions

1. Does every Christian have a vocation, or only those in "ministry"?
2. How did this chapter redefine your understanding of the relationship of work and ministry? How can you see your work as a ministry to the world?

3. How can you redirect your work toward God's design in Christ?

4. How should love for God and neighbor change the way you work?

How Should the Christian Live?

Greg Forster

PEOPLE OFTEN GRASP THAT GOD CARES ABOUT THEIR WORK, but are left asking: So what does that mean for me? How do I figure out what God wants me to do in my work? How do I handle struggles and disappointments? Should I quit my job if my boss is unethical or if my work environment is non-Christian? Should I try to steer clear of "ordinary" business jobs if I can, and find a nonprofit or parachurch organization where my work will serve a good cause?

We in the faith and work movement have struggled to provide guidance at that level. We know that every person, every calling, and every particular arena of service is different. It can be daunting to try to generalize.

As David Miller of the Princeton Faith and Work Initiative has said, it would be nice if we could get an e-mail from God every morning with His instructions for the day. But that's not how He's chosen to work. He's given us biblical teaching and He has built up the faith community; let's turn to those resources and see what He has for us.

Take Comfort, Then Get out of Your Comfort Zone

If we are in Christ, the first thing God offers for our work is comfort. Let's be honest: work creates a lot of anxiety. Am I doing what God wants? How do I face affliction and ethical uncertainty? What if I lose my job?

Jesus is with you to give you all the grace and power you need to do whatever He calls you to do. Jesus is not distant, high up in the sky, gazing down on a faraway world. That's not Jesus, that's Zeus.

The same Jesus who ascended to heaven, saying, "all authority has been given to me in heaven and earth," also said "remember, I am with you always, to the end of the age" (Matt. 28:18, 20). In

Paul's affliction, he says: "My grace is sufficient for you" (2 Cor. 12:9). In Paul's teaching, he says: "God is faithful; he will not allow you to be tempted beyond what you are able, but with the temptation he will also provide a way out so that you may be able to bear it" (1 Cor. 10:13). And when we fail, He says through His beloved disciple: "If we confess our sins, he is faithful and righteous to forgive us our sins and to cleanse us from all unrighteousness" (1 John 1:9).

By the power of the Holy Spirit, the same Jesus who is ruling the universe, working all things together for the good of those who love Him, is also inside us. He is with us, He knows all our troubles, He sympathizes with all our weaknesses, and He pours out grace and power to us through the Spirit.

This, by the way, is one reason the Trinity is so important. Only a three-personal God can be in heaven ruling the cosmos and inside us at the same time, and still be the same almighty God in both places. The Trinity is not abstract speculation; it's the daily reality we experience in our vocations!

Jesus will give you grace and power to face whatever His calling requires you to face. You may be called to spend most of your work doing tasks you dislike; Jesus will give you grace and power for that. You may be called to work for an arrogant, domineering boss; Jesus will give you grace and power for that. You may be called to work alongside dishonest, backbiting coworkers; Jesus will give you grace and power for that. You may be called to lose your job and have to find another opportunity to use your gifts productively; Jesus will give you grace and power for that.

On the other hand, you may be blessed with amazing opportunities. You may well have everything going for you! If so, Jesus will give you grace and power to take full advantage of those opportunities for His Kingdom. The more God invests in you, the more return on investment He expects you to be striving to give Him. That's the lesson of the parable of the talents.

He also provides wisdom. James says: "If any of you lacks wisdom, he should ask God—who gives to all generously and ungrudgingly—and it will be given him. But let him ask in faith" (James 1:5–6). We ask in prayer, in studying His Word, in worship and fellowship in the local church, and in counsel from spiritual leaders and friends He has brought into our lives.

Take comfort, but don't get too comfortable. Don't presume on His grace, assuming that because He will give grace and power you can just sit back and go with the flow. The more opportunities you have to advance God's Kingdom purposes through your work—serving your neighbors, supporting your household, going the extra mile for those who are in greatest need or vulnerability, and giving glory to the one God who rules all—the more you need to take those opportunities if you really want to follow God.

He will give grace and power, yes—and beware! Much is expected from those to whom much has been given.

Know Who You Are in Christ and
Who You Are in the World

This is why a gospel identity is so important. Only the gospel can empower you to work while removing the burden of *earning* from your work. In our vocations, God calls us to get out of our comfort zones, working hard to accomplish His purposes. But we rest on God's saving grace in the cross and the empty tomb of Christ for our standing and favor with God. We are not earning our place in the glorious Kingdom whose purposes we work so hard to advance.

That is why the high and holy calling of God is a blessing for us and not a curse. We know who we are in Christ. We know that God gives us this high calling because He loves us, because He has already adopted us as His children and secured a place in His Kingdom for us. There is no chance we will lose our real and ultimate blessing, however weak or deficient we may sometimes be in our vocations here.

We aren't earning in the Kingdom; we're learning in the Kingdom. We aren't just taking care of God's world in our vocations; we're learning how to be God's children. God is using our callings to shape us into the kind of people He wants His children to be. That's one reason it's sometimes quite difficult!

But you don't leave behind your natural human identity and relationships when you embrace your gospel identity and your relationship with Christ. Even after Paul became the world's greatest missionary, he continued to claim both his Jewish identity and his identity as a Roman citizen. He had relationships with people that helped make him the person he was. Jesus didn't replace those relationships; He suffused them with His grace and power to Paul.

In the same way, you are more than just a Christian. You are many other things as well—perhaps a husband or wife, perhaps a mother or father, perhaps an employee or student, perhaps a coworker, perhaps a citizen. Hopefully you are a church member. And whatever else you are, you are certainly a neighbor to all those God brings into your life!

The intersection between our gospel identity and our natural identities—our relationship with Christ and our relationships with those around us—is where we find most of the challenges and opportunities of our vocations. In my case, I'm called to be a good husband and father and church member; a good employee to my supervisors and to the school that employs me, as well as a good employer to those I supervise; a good craftsman to those who receive the services I provide (including you, the reader of this book!); a good citizen to my city, state, and country; and much else besides. These identities reveal to me much of my calling from God.

See the Big Picture, but Don't "Despise Small Things"

Hopefully you are beginning to see how central relationships are to God's design for us as human beings and the way we follow His calling in our lives. God made us to be relational—"it is not good that man should be alone" is the only "not good" pronounced before the Fall. We are made male and female in the image of God, made from the beginning to be fellow workers and family members, so we could show the world through our relationships with one another what the divine nature looks like: the holy love of three persons for each other, together forever as one God.

That, by the way, is another reason the Trinity is important. The unitarian God of Islam and of Christian heresy is eternally isolated and alone. The Trinitarian God is a relational being and makes us for relationship, to show His holy love through our vocations.

No one works alone. Your work is extensively bound up with the work of all the people around you—the boss you work for, the coworkers you work with, the customers you serve, the household your work supports, the people you buy things from using the money you make in your job. And all their work is in turn bound up with the work of thousands of others. Ultimately, your work is interdependent with the work of millions around the world.

Suppose you work on an assembly line making a part that goes into the braking system of a car. If all you see is the machine you operate on the assembly line and your paycheck, you're missing the big picture. You are making cars safer, saving lives. You serve the customer (drivers) and your community, making God's world more like what He wants it to be. That's your first contribution to the big picture.

Now go a step further. Why does your company pay you to operate that machine on the assembly line? Because customers want cars to be safer, so they're willing to pay a little more for better brakes—including that little part you make. The company pays you because your work creates value for it.

Now keep going. The paycheck you make for creating value for your employer supports your household. The goods and services you purchase with that paycheck allow other workers to do their work, serving the world in all their various ways and supporting their own households.

Maybe you don't get a paycheck for doing your job. You could be a homemaker or a retiree. All the same things still apply to you, though—you do work (in the home, volunteering, etc.) that serves people and makes the world a better place. Your work contributes to the well-being of your household and community, and helps other people do their work. You're no less part of God's big picture; the paychecks are not the point, they're just useful tools for keeping things going.

Hopefully now you can see that "the big picture" is not something that happens apart from the ordinary tasks of everyday life. Those mundane tasks are precisely where the big picture happens. That's why the Bible is constantly stressing faithfulness and conscientiousness in performing our routine duties. That's where God paints the big picture!

Zechariah rebukes "whoever has despised the day of small things." He tells them they will change their tune when they realize that the "eyes of the LORD . . . scan throughout the whole earth" (Zech. 4:10). Even on the assembly line, or in the kitchen at home, or in the cab of a truck, or in an office cubicle!

360-Degree Productivity

Time to get down to brass tacks. The main purpose of work is to be productive—what the Bible calls "fruitful." Our work should create value for others.

That means work is fundamentally about love. Because we will spend more waking hours engaged in work than any other activity, work is the main way we carry out the Great Commandment to love God and neighbor. That commandment is our touchstone; it should shape our thinking about what it means to work fruitfully. Am I working to glorify God and for the good of my neighbors?

The first part of the Great Commandment brings us to an important point. When I say work should create value, I don't mean fake value, like the "value" people get out of pornography or frivolous and wasteful luxuries, but real value. We are to provide goods and services that God says are valuable, caring for people's needs and helping God's world flourish.

In other words, in our work, we must first and foremost love God, must serve God as His stewards. Our work must be productive—fruitful—for God. He has called on us to be good stewards of His world through our work, and that's our first test of productivity.

But remember what we said before about gospel identity and natural identity? Our relationship with God plays out in our relationships with all those around us. While God takes first place, we do not love and serve Him separately from loving and serving others. We love and serve Him primarily by loving and serving others.

That means 360-degree productivity. Think about that "big picture" that plays itself out in the "small things" Zechariah talked about. Our work is an opportunity to be fruitful for a wide variety of people, all at the same time!

We want to love and be fruitful for our customers or clients—whoever is served by our work. We want to love and be fruitful for our households, supporting them and maintaining their well-being. We want to love and be fruitful for our employers, being good employees and creating value for the organization.

In practice this involves knowing how the particular kind of work we do creates value for the world. What is God's purpose for the sector of the economy in which I work, and the profession or occupation I belong to? And it means integrating, not "balancing," our lives in and out of the home.

We should also be on the lookout for ways to be especially fruitful for the poor and the vulnerable, not by condescending and patronizing but by seeking protection and restoration. How can we love and serve our fellow stewards who are facing the biggest challenges in fulfilling their stewardship role?

Be Ready to Persevere and Ready to Innovate

There's too much happy talk in the faith and work movement. Yes, it's important for us to understand that glorifying our marvelous God by serving Him and our neighbors through our daily labor is a beautiful and mighty supernatural wonder. Who can find words to express what an honor it is that God should choose us to care for His world, and then descend to give us grace and power to do it?

But the everyday reality of work for most people is hard. It's often painful. It's often dark. People work in the midst of toil, frustration, and injustice. As He did on the cross, so He does in our many arenas of service today—He does His most sublime works not apart from the depths of worldly depravity, but by working in and through those depths to lift up His own glory in His holy and unconditional love for us.

To be faithful in your work, you will need to persevere through suffering. Over and over and over again in the Bible, we are told that perseverance through suffering is one of the most important ways God refines us into the kind of children He wants us to be. "Dear friends, don't be surprised when the fiery ordeal comes among you to test you as if something unusual were happening to you," says Peter (1 Pet. 4:12). The workplace is no exception.

That doesn't mean, however, that we have to take the world exactly as it comes to us and simply tough it out—just put up with it. We are here to make a difference in this world. And we have Christian liberty to follow God through our bad situations to a point where we can leave them, when He gives the opportunity. The same Paul who told slaves "obey your human masters" (Eph. 6:5) also said, "if you can become free, by all means take the opportunity" (1 Cor. 7:21). After all, the cross is followed by the empty tomb!

The freedom to innovate, the freedom to be creative and seek opportunities to do new and different things, is also essential to dealing with ethical challenges at work. When you are called upon to do something that isn't right, in most cases you are not facing a flat choice between obeying or quitting. Very often you can use the creative gifts God gave you to find a way to keep both your job and your integrity. Your answer to the unethical order might be neither "yes" nor "no," but, "How about if we tried it this way?"

Perseverance and creativity are also essential to bearing witness to Christ at work. In our pluralistic culture, Christians are no longer entitled to assume our neighbors are open to hearing from us. Moreover, some businesses are unsure of what anti-discrimination laws require of them (the courts keep changing their minds) so they will often discourage proactive evangelism.

In this environment, a Christian worker needs to earn the right to be heard through diligent perseverance and creative innovation, doing excellent work and creating value for everyone in the workplace. Until you have had a chance to show that you are a valuable coworker, it is appropriate to be more reserved (although openings can be taken as they arise). The worker who has been in the same workplace for years and has a track record of glorifying Christ through his work can afford to stretch further in talking about Him.

Know When to Hold 'Em and Know When to Fold 'Em

We can't talk about work without talking about when not to work. God calls us not only to work, but to stop working. The two most important occasions to stop are rest and protest.

"He gives sleep to the one he loves," says the psalmist, and it's true! We aren't God, we're God's creatures—made with limits, and made to rest when we reach our limits. The psalmist rebukes our tendency to continue in business, or just in busyness, when God would have us rest: "In vain you get up early and stay up late, working hard to have enough food—yes, he gives sleep to the one he loves" (Ps. 127:2).

In Genesis, God's creation of the world is described as work, and that's a radical break from the pagan religions whose gods do no work. But each creative declaration ("let there be . . . let there be . . .") is followed by a moment of beholding ("God saw . . . God saw . . .") and appreciation ("it was good . . . it was good . . ."). And the six days of work in Genesis 1 are followed by a day of rest in Genesis 2.

We are called to reproduce this pattern. It doesn't necessarily have to be six parts work for every one part rest, although those proportions are at least suggestive. But we must regularly "down tools" and receive our rest from God's hand in appreciation of how good He is and all the good He's done for us. We do this each night, and we do it supremely in corporate worship on the Lord's Day.

If you find it difficult to stop working and set your daily labors out of your mind—or to stop surfing the web or doing whatever else you do to occupy the time—consider this an invitation to discipline yourself to rest for God. Lay down the burden of needing to work or stay busy. He gives to His beloved sleep.

While we're on the subject of stopping work, if you are employed in a job, let me also invite you to consider where your ethical boundaries are. What might your employer call on you to do that would force you to quit your job if no creative way around it could be found? As our cultural environment becomes more pluralistic, this question will become more important for Christians to consider. And when the crisis comes, it will be too late to form a carefully considered opinion. The time to think calmly and rationally about the tough questions is now. Every Christian should know, before the time comes, the kinds of situations under which he or she would walk away or resign.

Don't Go It Alone—Even the Lone Ranger Had Tonto

I know all this is a lot to take on. That's why our great God has made us in His image for relationship with others, to rely on one another's love! You are surrounded by potential sources of support; God has placed them there for a reason.

Above all, of course, rely on God Himself. As James says, ask for wisdom in faith. Discipline yourself in prayer, Bible study, worship, and other practices to seek and know His will. Rely on your family. Rely on your pastor and your church community. Rely on spiritual leaders and fellow Christians. They are a source of wisdom, comfort, encouragement, and accountability.

Consider, also, how you might join with other Christians in similar vocational situations—those who do the same kind of work or face challenges and opportunities similar to yours. "How can *I* be a faithful worker in *my* arena of service?" is a daunting question. "How can *we* be faithful workers in *our* arena of service?" is much more encouraging. That, again, is how God made us! And it is through such vocational communities that the Holy Spirit is most apt to bring His grace and power to the distinct needs of each vocation.

Local churches and other Christian communities can also draw Christians together from different kinds of vocations to advance God's purposes in the world. Rather than just giving money, why not organize a project that puts people's talents to use meeting unmet needs in your community? Amy Sherman's book *Kingdom Calling* provides a wealth of guidance and inspiration for such initiatives.

Be Satisfied without Slacking; Content but Not Complacent

I began with the idea that we take comfort without getting comfortable. If we stay grounded in that idea, the end result is an amazing thing. It is something that is not naturally possible for people, but becomes possible for us through the miraculous power of the Holy Spirit.

We should hope to experience a deep sense of spiritual satisfaction with our lives—a sense that we are living a life worth living, the kind of life God made us to live. But that satisfaction does not create slacking. It is precisely as we follow God actively, using our creative gifts to innovate, relying on Him to persevere, that we reach this satisfaction. It is strenuous activity that creates this serenity; we can rest spiritually because we work in the Spirit.

Resting in the satisfaction that we are living the lives God made us for, knowing that God will always give us the grace and power to follow our callings, we can stop chasing security and reputation and sex and power and money and stuff. The secret of life is to be content with the presence and provision of God, as we have come to know and trust Him through the gospel. This presence and provision comes to us both as we follow our vocations and as we rest from them, and worship the One from whom they come.

Discussion Questions

1. How can you take comfort knowing that Jesus provides grace and power for every situation? Where do you need grace and power in your work right now?
2. How is your work tied into the bigger picture?
3. Are you working to glorify God and serve your neighbors? How can your work be leveraged toward these two ends?
4. Whom might you connect with better for mutual support in following God through your daily work?

4

How Should the Church Engage?

Tom Nelson

A person should think of us in this way: as servants of
Christ and managers of the mysteries of God. In this
regard, it is required that managers be found faithful.
—1 Corinthians 4:1–2

CONFESSION IS GOOD FOR THE SOUL. BUT LET'S BE HONEST,
it's hard for pastors. Making a heartfelt confession before my
congregation was very hard, yet would prove transformative for
our faith community.

Pastoral Malpractice

Pastoral malpractice may seem a rather severe self-assessment, but I could not find a more accurate description of my vocational failure. The inconvenient truth I could not evade, ignore, or dismiss was the harsh reality that although I was called to equip my congregation for all of life, I had only been equipping them for a small sliver of their lives. I had given little sustained thought to the activities my parishioners spent so much time doing throughout the week.

Thinking back on it, I certainly believed my congregation's work mattered. I was especially aware of this during the offering time on Sunday or in the midst of a capital campaign. But at some point, I realized that the thing that actually mattered most to me was my own work, measured by things such as the numerical growth of the attendance at our Sunday services. I may not have said so explicitly, but I was living as if my vocation as a pastor was far more important than the vocations of my parishioners.

The Majority-Minority Disparity

My pastoral malpractice can best be summed up as a professionally accepted, yet blinding vocational failure, embedded in a majority-minority disparity. In other words, I had been spending the majority of my time equipping congregants for things they were called to do with a minority of their time. Without malice and with good intention, my pastoral vocational paradigm had been informed by a theological deficiency. At the heart of it all, I had failed to see clearly—from Genesis to Revelation—the high importance of vocation and the integral theological connections of faith, work, and economics.

Somehow I had missed how the gospel speaks into every nook and cranny of life, connecting Sunday worship with Monday work in a seamless fabric of Holy Spirit-empowered faithfulness. With the best of intentions but with far-reaching negative ramifications, I had been perpetuating a large Sunday-to-Monday gap in my preaching, discipleship, and pastoral care. It was time to embrace some desperately needed change.

The Sunday-to-Monday Gap

I am discovering I am not alone in my pastoral malpractice. For many pastors and Christian leaders, there is a large Sunday-to-Monday gap. This gap leads to a deficient understanding of the integral relationship between worship on Sunday and work on Monday. Many well-intentioned pastors spend the majority of their time equipping their congregations for what church members do with only a minority of their time. And this ignores the importance of everyday work and the workplaces Christians inhabit so many hours each week. The negative consequences of this common form of pastoral malpractice are both striking and sobering.

What Is Really at Stake?

I remember a preaching professor in seminary saying, *"If there is a mist in the pulpit there is a fog in the pew."* While my homiletics professor was driving home the importance of sermon clarity, his wise words also speak to pastoral leadership flowing from the pastoral pulpit. While a mist of confusion in the pulpit is far-reaching, my professor never talked about the perilous consequences that follow when there is not merely a mist in the pulpit, but instead a thick, blinding, and mind-numbing fog. What does it mean for a congregation when a pastoral leader is foggy in his theology of the relationship between faith, work, and economics? What are the consequences of serving as a pastor with an impoverished theological and vocational paradigm?

Grasping the full and far-reaching effects of a pastor failing to connect Sunday-to-Monday with an integral whole-life discipleship mission is beyond the scope of this chapter. However, it is fair and reasonable to conclude that a thick pastoral fog cannot be a good recipe for congregational flourishing and cultural influence. I have become increasingly convinced through both my own personal experience as well as my conversations with many pastoral colleagues that the Sunday-to-Monday gap is much wider, more prominent, and more perilous than we care to admit. So what is really at stake? What is at stake is the rightful worship of God, the spiritual formation of God's people, gospel plausibility, gospel proclamation, and the furtherance of the common good.

The Rightful Worship of God

If church members see Sunday morning as the primary time they worship God and do not understand that what they do on Monday morning is prime-time worship, then our good and great Triune God who is worthy of our true and best worship receives puny and impoverished worship from His new covenant people. In the original creation, God designed us to work and worship in a seamless way. Clearly there was no Sunday-to-Monday gap. While we are not to worship our work (for that is idolatry), we are to see the work we do, though presently marred by sin and now redeemed by the gospel, as an act of worship done unto God for His glory and the good of others (Col. 3:23). In the saving grace of Christ and through the indwelling power of the Holy Spirit, apprentices of Jesus live and work before an Audience of One in a seamless life of worship.

Spiritual Formation of Congregants

If we perpetuate a Sunday-to-Monday gap, our efforts at spiritual formation—leading followers of Jesus into increasing Christlikeness—will be incomplete. If congregants see their spiritual formation as primarily something that occurs on Sunday or as a certain spiritual discipline they do during the week, then their spiritual growth is greatly hindered. The work we are called to do every day is one of the primary means the Holy Spirit uses to conform us into the image of Christ.

We shape our work and our work shapes us. It infuses a sense of experiential meaning in our daily lives. The Swiss psychiatrist and Holocaust survivor, Viktor Frankl, concluded that humans find a sense of meaning not only in the relationships we forge, but also in and through the work we do.[34] That is truly a remarkable insight. Yet many followers of Jesus enter a church every Sunday feeling like second-class citizens. They listen to sermons which implicitly, and sometimes even explicitly, communicate that the everyday work of laypersons is insignificant because it lacks the intrinsic meaning and importance of ministerial, or "spiritual" work.

Gospel Plausibility

If the congregations of our local churches are not equipped to connect Sunday-to-Monday, then our gospel witness will be neither persuasive nor compelling to the broader culture. Sociologist James Hunter makes a strong case for the unique faith contours of our present cultural context. According to Hunter, both the great dissolution of faith as well as the profound differences that separate the myriad faiths in our increasingly pluralistic world foster greater implausibility for the uniqueness, truth, importance, and believability of Christian faith.[35] The gospel we cherish not only needs winsome and persuasive proclamation in our increasingly secular cultural context, it also needs daily incarnation. We must present a visible demonstration of what a gospel-centered life looks like, and one of the primary ways we do this is in and through the messy and broken workplaces God's people inhabit each and every day.

It is in and through our daily work that colleagues who are not yet Christ followers have the opportunity to see the gospel's transforming truth lived out. In this way, Christians bear witness both in the quality of work we do and by the attitude with which we approach our work. In His most famous sermon, Jesus reminds us that we are to be salt and light in the world, not only by what we say to others, but by what others see in us. It is our good works that speak to others. Our Spirit-driven actions point those around us to the good God we love and serve. And these good works are not merely reserved for religious acts of piety, but encompass the good work we do every day. Dorothy Sayers speaks with perceptive clarity when she asserts, "The only Christian work is good work well done."[36] Our vocational faithfulness, lived out with common grace, makes the gospel plausible. It is in the good works of faithful Christians that the gospel of grace finds fertile soil.

Gospel Proclamation

If our congregations are not equipped to connect Sunday-to-Monday, our collective proclamation of the gospel to this lost and dying world is muted. Many of our congregants spend a great deal of time in their workplaces each week. So it is not difficult to see that it is this environment that harbors the greatest potential for gospel witness. The workplace represents one of our best opportunities to see the gospel create real transformation and life change. Are we encouraging and equipping our congregants to share their Christian faith with their coworkers? Do we grasp that a primary work of the church is the church at work? Bill Peel points out with prophetic clarity, "God calls every Christian to be a witness for Him. So for most of us, our mission field is where we spend the bulk of our time: the workplace."[37] What would our churches look like if our members saw their primary gospel mission field as the workplace they go to every day?

Furtherance of the Common Good

If we don't seek to better connect Sunday-to-Monday, then the common good of all peoples is underserved and human culture is impoverished. The gospel compels us to actively seek and continually further the well-being of all God's image-bearers, regardless of whether or not they have yet put their faith in Christ.

Writing to the exiles in Babylon, the prophet Jeremiah admonishes God's covenant people to seek the common good. He writes, "Pursue the well-being of the city I have deported you to. Pray to the LORD on its behalf, for when it thrives, you will thrive" (Jer. 29:7).

What does seeking the welfare of a city entail? Jeremiah helps us with this important question when he encourages God's covenant people not to form an isolated cultural ghetto, but to get married, have children, work hard, and robustly engage in the economic life of the city of Babylon.

It is not insignificant that Babylon was a thoroughly pagan city with an abundance of idol worship, gross sin, and untethered evil. Yet even in spite of such a godless context, God's covenant people are called to pray for the city and live holy lives in the midst of a very unholy place while yet seeking the good of their neighbors. As followers of Jesus, we are called and empowered by the Holy Spirit to bloom where we are planted. As we live fruitful lives in our vocations and steward well our work in the Babylonian marketplaces of our time, not only are we recipients of God's blessings, those around us also flourish as they enjoy the very tangible blessings of common grace. The writer of Proverbs puts it this way, "When the righteous thrive, a city rejoices" (Prov. 11:10). As we indwell a common grace for the common good, our congregants become inviting signposts to the saving grace of Christ.

Narrowing the Sunday-to-Monday Gap

Are you seeing the grave peril of the Sunday-to-Monday gap? Do you realize that the true worship of God, the spiritual formation of followers of Jesus, the plausibility of the gospel, the proclamation of the gospel, and the furtherance of the common good are all on the line? So how do we begin to narrow the Sunday-to-Monday gap? I believe we must become more intentional in teaching a robust theology of vocation that informs our people's work.

In our corporate worship services, we must cultivate a liturgical regularity that affirms our people's daily work. As pastors we must also make a more concerted effort to relationally invest in the vocations of our church members, celebrating and applauding their daily work.

A Robust Theology that Informs Work

The heart cry of so many Christians I speak to is, "Pastor, does my work matter? I know your work matters, but does what I do every day matter to God and matter in the world?" When missionaries and pastors are celebrated for their callings, many congregants believe their vocational callings are unimportant. Many feel like second-class citizens in the church because they have not been taught the robust theology of vocation that the Bible clearly and compellingly teaches.

After a long, exhausting day at the office or on the way home from the tiring clamor of the workshop, many congregants face melancholy moments of reflection. Whether they have achieved the pinnacle of career success or have experienced the deep valleys of job failure, a sense of emptiness often haunts them: "Is there more to life than this? How does my gospel faith speak into what I do each and every day?" Unable to answer these musings of the soul adequately, it is easy for many to settle for a conveniently compartmentalized life where Sunday faith and Monday work remain worlds apart. But this dualistic approach is not the path to human flourishing.

The good news is that the Bible speaks about a flourishing, integrated existence, not an impoverished, bifurcated, or compartmentalized life. It is not surprising then that the Bible speaks a great deal about the jobs we are called to do. From Genesis to Revelation, three transforming truths emerge that can help Christians close the Sunday-to-Monday gap and bring greater glory to God and greater gospel coherence to life.

Created with Work in Mind

First, we were created with work in mind. In Genesis 1 our Creator is introduced as a God who works. The Bible begins with the words: "In the beginning God created the heavens and the earth." We then discover as humans we have been created in a working God's image: "So God created man in his own image;

he created him in the image of God; he created them male and female" (Gen. 1:27). Being an image-bearer means many things, yet an essential aspect of bearing God's image is in and through the work we do every day. This foundational aspect of God's design for human beings is evident in the Creation Mandate: "God blessed them and God said to them, 'Be fruitful, multiply, fill the earth, and subdue it. . . .'" (Gen. 1:28). God's command reflects His design and desire that we would be "fruitful." The Hebrew word translated as "fruitful" brings with it both the idea of procreativity and productivity.[38] At the heart of God's design for us is the calling to be productive in our work. This truth is reinforced strongly in Genesis 2 where Adam is placed in the garden with a twofold vocational job description, namely "to work it and watch over it" (v. 15).

Though our present work is a mixed bag of the good and the bad, the fulfilling and the frustrating, work was an integral part of God's design even before sin and death entered the world. To be human is more than being a worker, but work is at the heart of our intended place and purpose within creation. Work as God designed it at creation must be seen as contribution and not merely compensation. From cradle to grave, God designed us to contribute to both His good world and the common good whether or not we receive a paycheck. The biblical definition of work is about much more than that which we get paid to do.

Throughout the book of Genesis, we observe that God designed work and worship to be seamless, not separated or fragmented. In God's original design there was no Sunday-to-Monday gap. While we are not to worship our work, we must understand that our work is one of the primary ways we worship God.[39] The integral and seamless design we see in Genesis 1–2 is followed by the massive disintegration of God's perfect design in chapter 3. Sin, death, and brokenness enter God's good world and badly vandalize and distort all aspects of the work of our hands. The fruitfulness of procreativity and productivity are now negatively affected. Adam and Eve had to deal with thorns and thistles of work and so do we.

Jesus the Carpenter

The second transforming truth is that in Christ we are redeemed and empowered to work for the glory of God and the common good. The gospel shines the light of truth and grace that redeems the worker, but it also redeems the work we do and the workplaces we inhabit. Many of us tend to forget that Jesus spent the majority of His time on this sin-ravaged planet in a carpenter's shop working in obscurity with sawdust on His sinless hands and sweat on His holy brow. Biblical scholars often refer to this period of Jesus' life, from roughly ages twelve to thirty, as the hidden years. While the gospel writers don't tell us much about these years, we must not see them as unimportant to Jesus' incarnational and redemptive mission.

The gospel writer Mark points to Jesus' hidden years by noting the revealing thoughts of the residents of His hometown, "Isn't this the carpenter, the son of Mary and the brother of James, Joses, Judas, and Simon? And aren't his sisters here with us?" (Mark 6:3). Jesus' mission, to die on a blood-stained cross to bear our sin and satisfy the wrath of a holy, righteous God, is always primary. But the fact that the incarnate Son of God spent so much time working with His hands, in a carpenter's shop, speaks to the centrality and importance of work.[40] It is an essential part of our humanity. Jesus honored His heavenly Father both in the carpentry shop and on the cross. Jesus, the craftsman carpenter, affirmed the dignity of human work and demonstrated how the work we are called to do is an act of worship and loving service to others.

The Protestant Reformers of the sixteenth century not only recovered the gospel, they also recognized faithful vocational stewardship as an imperative based on Jesus' teaching on the Great Commandment (Matt. 22:37–39). Loving our neighbor rightly was understood first and foremost as doing our work rightly. We must realize the work we are called to do, whatever that may be, is a vital aspect of loving God and loving our neighbor. Jesus the carpenter, who worked diligently, rightly invites us to enter His easy yoke and learn from Him (Matt. 11:28–30).

Learning from Jesus includes following His example in the way we work each and every day.

Worshipful Work

A third transforming truth is that we are to worship God in and through our work. Our work matters, but it can matter too much. What God designed as an act of worship can become an idol in our lives. Work idolatry often evidences itself when we find our identity in our work rather than in our relationship with Christ. Work idolatry is also seen when we live overextended, stress-filled lives that fail to embrace regular Sabbath rest.

The apostle Paul who embraced a seamless gospel faith of work and rest writes, "I have been crucified with Christ, and I no longer live, but Christ lives in me. The life I now live in the body, I live by faith in the Son of God, who loved me and gave himself for me" (Gal. 2:20). The apostle Paul who calls us to a new life of gospel faith also speaks of how saving faith in Christ transforms our work into God-honoring, Christ-exalting worship. Writing to the church at Colossae, Paul urges us to do our work well and for the glory of God. "Whatever you do, do it from the heart, as something done for the Lord and not for people" (Col. 3:23).

The work of our congregants matters more than we often realize. The work they are called to do is a primary means of their worship and it is a large contributor to their spiritual formation. Faithfulness in vocational stewardship also prepares our congregants for the good work they will one day perform in the new heavens and new earth. In His parable of the talents, Jesus strongly affirms the earthly money managers who were faithful in their work. Jesus says, "Well done, good and faithful servant! You were faithful over a few things; I will put you in charge of many things. Share your master's joy" (Matt. 25:23). The work our parishioners do now is a seedbed of preparation for their work in the future. Every Monday morning they arrive at a job that is infused with profound eternal significance.

Are we helping our congregants grasp just how much God cares about their work? Are we equipping those entrusted to our care to see their work as God sees it? Are we helping them fight the sinful gravitational tug toward work idolatry or work slothfulness? Are we coming alongside our church members and helping them discover what faithful vocational stewardship looks like? Do our congregants see their work and workplace as a primary means of their spiritual formation and gospel mission? What steps do you need to take in your local church to teach a more seamless gospel faith that narrows the Sunday-to-Monday gap?

A Liturgical Regularity that Affirms Work

Closing the Sunday-to-Monday gap is not only about helping people connect what they profess to believe with how they work on Monday, it is also about intentionally bringing their Monday world into our Sunday worship celebrations. Regardless of our liturgical and ecclesiastical traditions, when a pastor or Christian leader embraces a more robust theology of vocation, it will seamlessly seep into corporate worship planning and execution.

Transformed Preaching

Sermon preparation will gain a heightened awareness of the strong thread of work woven throughout the biblical canon. Many pastors will choose to preach a focused series on faith and work. A sermon series on economics and the common good should also be considered.[41]

In addition to a sermon series, the topics of work and vocational stewardship should regularly find their way into sermon preparation. The *Theology of Work Bible Commentary* is a helpful sermon preparation tool for the serious expositor of Holy Scripture.[42] Sermons will note the work themes present in the biblical text and apply the truth to the various work contexts of members of the congregation. Sermon illustrations will feature workplace settings, including the challenges and opportunities they bring. Pastors will regularly teach how the gospel speaks into Monday life, and their sermons will avoid dichotomous language (such as "the sacred" and "the secular") that suggests a hierarchy of vocational callings. Using language to describe pastors, missionaries, and para-church staff as "full-time Christian workers" should also be avoided. Such verbiage projects an undue elevation of certain vocational callings and diminishes the significance of others.

Congregational Songs and Hymnody

A hopeful and robust theology of vocation is not only expressed in our preaching, but also celebrated in congregational singing. Greater attentiveness and intentionality to song lyrics is needed by those charged with planning corporate worship services. Sadly, some well-established hymnody of the church actually reinforces a dualistic Sunday-to-Monday gap, rather than affirming a more integrated understanding of gospel faith. The song "Turn Your Eyes Upon Jesus" has many good lyrics, but it also has problematic lyrics such as, 'the things of earth will grow strangely dim in the light of his glory and grace.' These lyrics subtly diminish the importance of the created world, reinforce unbiblical dualism, and distance gospel faith from Monday-morning work duties and responsibilities. On the other hand, the hymn, "This Is My Father's World," while recognizing the present brokenness of the created world, rightly emphasizes the goodness of creation and the blessings of common grace.

Workplace Testimonies

Personal testimonies of gospel transformation offered up during a corporate worship service should include stories from congregants regarding their vocational stewardship and workplace mission. Testimonies should include those paid for their work, but also stay-at-home spouses, volunteers, and retirees whose vocational callings are not financially compensated. In my particular ecclesial context, we embrace a variety of both video and live testimonies. Testimonies can also take more of an interview format where the congregant is asked two or three brief questions followed by a pastoral prayer. The workplace testimony interview may include questions such as: "How would you describe your work?" "What do you find most fulfilling and most frustrating in your work?" "As an image-bearer of God, how does your work reflect God's work?" "How is the gospel shaping your work?" Few things are more encouraging and hope-inspiring to a congregation than hearing from other followers of Jesus in their church family who are called to similar vocations.

Pastoral Prayers, Commissionings, and Benedictions

Embracing a more robust theology of work should include pastoral prayers, pastoral commissioning, and benedictions. Pastoral prayers should address the brokenness of our world and the physical and emotional needs of congregants, but these prayers should also speak to the needs our people face in the workplace. Pastoral prayers will reflect in both tone and content a growing pastoral sensitivity to the relational difficulties, the stressful economic challenges, and the very complex ethical realities congregants face in their jobs. Pastoral prayers will speak into economic realities such as unemployment and underemployment. Pastoral prayers come before God asking divine assistance in workplace endurance, wisdom, strength, provision, and opportunity for gospel witness.

While the commissioning of missionaries and church workers will continue to be celebrated, other vocational callings will be celebrated too.

Often, corporate worship liturgies will include pastoral commissionings of various vocational sectors. With the beginning of a new school year, the vocational calling of teaching may be highlighted by affirming and commissioning all teachers within the congregation. Other times throughout the year, health care workers, government workers, blue-collar workers, other white-collar professionals, business owners, and students can be featured during the corporate worship gathering.

Pastoral benedictions will take on a new importance in the local church as well. Pastoral leaders will remind congregants as they leave that their vocational faithfulness is highly important to their discipleship and advancing God's mission in the world. Church members should understand that they represent and worship Christ each week in their workplaces (as the scattered church). The final words offered to a congregation in the corporate worship service play an important role in developing this understanding. A pastoral benediction from Psalms might include, "Let your work be seen by your servants, and your splendor by their children. Let the favor of the Lord our God be on us; establish for us the work of our hands—establish the work of our hands!" (Ps. 90:16–17).

A Relational Investment that Applauds Work

It is not enough to enlighten our congregations with a robust theology of work, nor is it enough to affirm them with a more liturgical regularity. If we are going to be faithful to our pastoral vocation we must also embrace pastoral practices that applaud the work of our congregants. With the many demands the pastoral vocation brings, we must prayerfully seek to make the connection between a reframed pastoral paradigm that equips people for whole-life discipleship and the need for reshaped pastoral priorities and practices.

I believe it is imperative that pastors assume a humble posture of curiosity toward the work our congregants perform. We should expand the breadth of our reading to include learning about their various vocations, but we should also carve out time to visit our congregants in their workplace settings. While certain workplaces will not be open to our presence, every vocation is open to our curiosity and learning. A regular reading diet of helpful guides such as the *Wall Street Journal, The Atlantic, Fast Company,* and *The Economist* will assist pastors to be current and conversant in the areas of business and the marketplace. In addition, specialized journals related to specific vocations can be consulted to gain greater understanding of the challenges facing other congregants. If we are committed to offering pastoral care and to equipping our congregants well for all of life, then the practice of regular workplace visits should be embraced with the same intentionality and sensitivity as hospital visits. Building regular workplace visits into my schedule has been one of the most transformative and important pastoral practices I have ever embraced.

Leading Organizational Change

Addressing the Sunday-to-Monday gap begins with you as a pastor or Christian leader, but it does not end there. For sustained transformation of your church culture, the broader leadership community of professional staff and congregational leaders must also recognize the peril of the Sunday-to-Monday gap and become catalysts for change. Of course this takes concerted prayer, gentle patience, and a long obedience in the same direction, but both pastoral faithfulness and faithful gospel mission are on the line. We must become patient, yet determined, Holy Spirit-empowered change agents for the local church. This is God's desire for us, and it is the hope of the world.

A Decade of Transformation

For over a decade the professional staff and church leaders whom I serve with have been working diligently to narrow the Sunday-to-Monday gap in our local church. Our Sunday worship services increasingly reflect the reality that the gospel speaks to and transforms all of life, including our work. We continue to press into how the gospel speaks to neighborly love, wealth creation, wise financial management, and economic flourishing.

We are still learning and unlearning as we go, doing our best to navigate what it means to embrace an integral gospel-centered faith and to narrow the Sunday-to-Monday gap.

My heart is increasingly encouraged when I receive an e-mail from a CEO or a stay-at-home mom or a student or a retiree in our congregation who has learned to see their Monday lives through the transforming lens of the biblical theology of vocation. As a pastor, I find increasing joy for my congregants who now embrace their paid and non-paid work as an offering to God, an opportunity for gospel witness, and a contribution to the common good. Many of my parishioners have a bigger bounce in their step and a new shout in their souls. For them, the gospel has become amazingly coherent and incredibly compelling. They experience this in their own lives and they also share it with others in various vocational settings and spheres of influence throughout the week.

A Newly Remodeled Congregation

With our kids growing up and heading off to college, my wife, Liz, knew it was time for a major remodel in our kitchen. At first, I was a bit reluctant. Our kitchen seemed just fine. I had grown accustomed to our kitchen with its green countertops. It was the only kitchen I knew. I couldn't help but think of the large chunk of change this remodel would require. Yet, my wife Liz saw something I couldn't see. Thankfully, I listened to Liz and we forged ahead with the project.

I will never forget when I saw our remodeled kitchen for the first time. The kitchen was beautifully designed and wonderfully welcoming. As I stared at our remodeled kitchen, I realized how drab our old kitchen was. How had I not seen it? How had I been so unaware?

The best way I know how to describe this past decade is that our congregation has undergone a major remodeling project. Looking back, I can't imagine how I had served for so long with such an impoverished pastoral paradigm. The newly remodeled congregation I serve is far more beautiful in its expression and more effective in its disciple-making mission. I now enjoy much greater job satisfaction knowing I am being a more faithful pastor. Confession of pastoral malpractice is good for the soul and it may very well be good for you and your congregation.

Discussion Questions

1. Where do you see evidence of the Sunday-to-Monday gap in your local church or your own discipleship?
2. Why is the Sunday-to-Monday gap so perilous to gospel-shaped ministry and a disciple-making mission?
3. How can you begin to close the Sunday-to-Monday gap in your church? In your own life?
4. Have you ever been taught that "regular work" is inferior to ministry work? How does it make you feel to know that the Bible actually teaches that all work is equally important and glorious, if it is done to God's glory?

What Does the Culture Say?

Daniel Darling

"PASTOR, I WISH I COULD GET UP EVERY DAY AND DO WORK for the Kingdom like you do." This sentiment is something I've heard countless times over the course of my ministry life. On the one hand, I value the evangelistic passion that burns in the heart of Christian laymen. On the other, I am saddened to hear such an impoverished doctrine of vocation.

For most Christians, there is a dichotomy between what they do on Sunday and the work they perform on Monday. One is Jesus work and the other is just . . . work. There are sociological and historical reasons for this way of thinking, but mostly it is because we pastors have not done a good enough job communicating the beauty of work as a gift from a good God. As a result, working Christians have imbibed some false ideas about their Monday through Friday experience.

Work Means Nothing

For many people, work is simply a means to an end. We need money to live. The way we get money is by working. Perhaps Johnny Paycheck, in his 1977 hit "Take This Job and Shove It," best embodied this utilitarian approach. According to a 2015 *Forbes* report on a Conference Board survey, more than 52 percent of Americans are unhappy at work. I suspect that some of this dissatisfaction is due to stagnating wages or poor work environments. Many workplaces can be demanding, soul-sucking prisons, where the only way to soldier on is to long for the weekend. But it could also be that work is drudgery because, for many, there seems to be no redeeming value in the work they do. It's show up, keep your nose clean, and produce for The Man.

Ironically, it's not simply nonreligious employees who see no value in their labor. Many, if not most, Christians see their workplaces as simple vehicles by which they can provide for their families, tithe their incomes to the church, and perhaps engage in occasional evangelistic conversations. The actual work seems unimportant in light of eternity. Sadly, this view is often buoyed by well-meaning, but reductionist messages heard every Sunday, where the pastor often implies that only church stuff matters to God. In calling people to sacrifice and give and pursue Christ, they send a subtle, but powerful message that what happens on Monday is unimportant.

I often felt this way growing up in church. My father is a plumber, who owned his own business for many years. He was a faithful elder and leader in the church. He gave enormous amounts of time for many important building projects. But I always got the sense, fueled by our church culture, that Dad was somehow on the Christian "junior varsity" squad. Pastors, missionaries, and anyone who received a paycheck from an evangelical 501(c)(3) were the real heroes. So-called laymen might be good men, useful for funding mission endeavors and lending their physical gifts to church projects, but less important than those tasked with preaching and teaching the Word. This dichotomy, prevalent in many Christian environments, is at odds with the view of work we see in Scripture.

From the very first pages of Scripture, we are presented with a God who works. The language of Genesis 1 and 2 pulsates with the rhythm of His creative activity: God designs; God commands; God acts. And each process is met by the affirmation: "And God saw that it was good."

Working. Creating. Cultivating. These are divinely ordered activities. They are good. But it's not simply God who creates. God also, we are told, creates unique creatures, which bear His image, who are also entrusted with creating and cultivating responsibilities.

While all of creation is spoken into existence, humans are deliberately crafted by the hands of God from the dust of the ground and endowed by God with the breath of life. Notice the ordering of the Genesis 1:26 account:

> Then God said, "Let us make man in our image,
> according to our likeness. They will rule the fish of
> the sea, the birds of the sky, the livestock, the whole
> earth, and the creatures that crawl on the earth."

God's first command, after creating humankind, is to delegate authority over creation to them, for its cultivation and flourishing. There is an unmistakable message in these creation accounts. Work is not something incidental to human existence, but part of the very design of creation. In between commands to assume authority over creation, to subdue (master) the raw resources of the earth, and to intentionally reproduce is the repeated phrase: "God created man in his image." It's as if God, through the divinely inspired authorship of Moses, is stamping upon this passage the idea: creating, working, cultivating are the ways in which humans most represent God in His world.

Furthermore, the text of Genesis insists that God created the world for His people to cultivate and image Him. Genesis 2:5 makes a statement about the raw and unfinished world before humans were present to cultivate it: "there was no man to work the ground," as if the ground, the soil, was created specifically to be cultivated by human beings. In Genesis 2:15, Moses writes that God "took the man and put him in the garden of Eden to work it and watch over it." Tom Nelson, pastor and author of *Work Matters*, writes:

> From Genesis 2 we see that the earth itself was created in order to be cultivated and shaped by humankind. Unspoiled pristine nature is not necessarily a preferred state. God desired that there would be harmonious human cooperation within the created order. Not only would the crown of creation have joyful intimacy with their creator, but they would also be given the joyful privilege of contributing to the work of God in his good world.[43]

Rather than being incidental to our purpose in the world, work is intrinsic to our calling as humans. We were created by the Creator to create. When we work, when we cultivate the raw materials of creation, when we develop and use our power and gifts wisely, we image God.

So why is it that many in society and even in the church have come to view work as merely a means to an end, rather than a good gift from a gracious God? I believe there are a few reasons.

We Are Subject to Sin's Curse on Work

While Genesis tells us the truth about work, about its design as a mandate from God for those who bear His image, it also tells us the story of how work, like the rest of creation, was corrupted by Adam's fall. The fruit that enticed the first couple bore poison, not simply for those who ate it, but for the entire cosmos. Listen as God speaks on the new reality of work:

> And he said to the man, "Because you listened to your wife and ate from the tree about which I commanded you, 'Do not eat from it': The ground is cursed because of you. You will eat from it by means of painful labor all the days of your life. It will produce thorns and thistles for you, and you will eat the plants of the field. You will eat bread by the sweat of your brow until you return to the ground, since you were taken from it. For you are dust, and you will return to dust." (Gen. 3:17–19)

Adam's sin spelled corruption and disintegration, not simply for humanity's relationship to God, but also for our relationship with the world around us. The once-beautiful creation is now tainted by the Fall and we no longer live at peace with God's good world. Tim Keller, pastor of Redeemer Presbyterian Church in New York City, writes:

> We were designed to know, serve, and love God supremely—and when we are faithful to that design, we flourish. But when we instead chose to live for ourselves, everything began to work backward. After this turning point, the human race began to live against the grain of the universe, against the grain of our own making and purpose.[44]

Work in a fallen world is still a means by which we bring glory to our Creator (Col. 3:23–24), but it is now met by a groaning creation (Rom. 8:22). The words of Jesus introduce the three-fold corruption of work: pain, frustration, and futility. Work is painful, not simply because of the exertion required. Even before the Fall, God established rhythms of work and rest. But what is different about labor in a corrupted cosmos is that work now brings pain. Most of us understand this. At times, hard work is fulfilling and exhilarating, but most often it makes us weary. Our bodies break down and seem unsuitable for our tasks.

There is also a frustration in our work. We are not simply cultivating gardens, we are battling the elements: thorns and thistles. The ground, once perfectly fertile in Eden, now fights back. And you don't have to be a farmer to feel the effects of the

Fall. Regardless of occupation, there seems to be a sense that we have to work twice as hard to be fruitful. Our thorns often appear in the form of sinful personality traits that pit employee against employee, difficult economic environments that keep us from reaching our full, creational potential, and natural corruptions in creation that seems to fight our every attempt to work it.

Last, our work is often corrupted by unfruitfulness. For many, even in prosperous Western democracies, work seems unfruitful. Economic injustices, market inequalities, and lack of opportunity often conspire to make even the most earnest effort at hard work seem unfruitful. A teacher labors against insurmountable odds to educate poor children in an inner-city environment, yet sees little fruit from her labors. An aid worker in a war-ravaged country's efforts seem to have no discernable impact on the death and disease around him. The public official tries, in vain, to reform the corrupt bureaucracy in her town.

There are times when, despite our best efforts to do good work, the corruption of our world overwhelms. At times the thorns and thistles choke out the fruitfulness. "Absolute futility," cried the writer of Ecclesiastes, of his meaningless life (Eccl. 1:2). Sometimes our frustrations are born out of the inability to use our gifts to their fullest potential. This is why those of us privileged to do work we enjoy should be thankful to dwell in pockets of God's common grace in the world. We must not forget that many people around the world daily experience the frustration of a corrupted cosmos.

So how can Christians find meaning in seemingly futile work? Of course there are always whispers of joy. Adversity, we are told, is God's chisel upon the character of our heart. And even seemingly meaningless work can, in the smallest way, contribute to the flourishing of those around us, even if we struggle to see this.

But there is a purpose to our work beyond these small victories. In Christ, we not only experience personal redemption by faith in His atoning sacrifice, but we experience the renewal of our original image-bearing purpose. Paul tells us in Ephesians 2 that the gospel restores God's people to the good works that God "prepared ahead of time" (v. 10). This is why we are exhorted to do our work "for the Lord" (Col. 3:22–23). And we are reminded that none of our labor, even the seemingly fruitless and futile, is in vain (1 Cor. 15:58).

In the resurrection, Christ reversed the curse of sin and death and renews what is futile in a disintegrating cosmos. For those who work "for the Lord," our image-bearing is being renewed, perfected, after the image of Christ. The work we do will endure into eternity, its worth not judged by present fruitfulness, but sifted by the refining fire of God's glory. The resurrection of Christ and our future resurrection means even the most meaningless, obscure, seemingly insignificant labors, when done for Christ, become trophies of grace (1 Cor. 3:10–13).

We Have Adopted a False Spiritual Dualism

In her landmark book, *Total Truth*, apologist Nancy Pearcey describes the "two-story" view of truth so prevalent in culture and even in the church. For evangelicals, this is often reflected in the way we view our work. We relegate faith, belief, and emotions to the upper story and locate more measurable things like work, science, and data in the lower story. The roots of this dualism in the larger culture can be traced to the Enlightenment, skepticism, Darwinism, and many other movements. In the church, there are roots in American revivalism and piety.

The bottom line is that many believers consider God's work to be limited to what we do on Sundays or any kind of evangelistic activity we might perform during the week. But our primary vocations are compartmentalized as a sort of necessary evil, a utilitarian tool enabling us to do God's work on Sundays.

Christians need to recover a more holistic view of their world. Dutch pastor and philosopher Abraham Kuyper summarized this holistic view in his well-known statement: "There is not a **square inch** in the whole domain of our human existence over which Christ, who is Sovereign over all, does not cry, 'Mine!'"[45]

How do we recover a view of Christ's Kingdom rule over our work? It begins by knowing, understanding, and teaching a full gospel. For many Christians, the gospel is understood as the transaction that takes place when they put their faith in Christ for salvation. The gospel is this transaction, but it is so much more. Hugh Whelchel writes in his book *How Then Should We Work?*: "Christians do not fully comprehend the biblical concepts of work, calling, and vocation because we have lost the vision of the grand metanarrative of the Bible." Whelchel continues:

> While sin and salvation are undeniable realities, they are not the complete gospel. In this abridged version of the gospel, Christianity becomes all about *us*. The Two-Chapter Gospel ignores creation and the final restoration. It leaves out God's reason for our creation and the Christian's final destination.[46]

In the Gospels, we see Jesus declare, often, that His presence on earth—His life, His death, and His resurrection—was the inauguration of His Kingdom, the fulfillment of God's promises delivered through His prophets in the Old Testament.

This is why Jesus declares, for instance, in Mark 1:15: "repent, for the kingdom of God is at hand." In one sense, the kingdom of God was already present in God's eternal sovereign kingly rule over His creation and His people (Ps. 103), but in another sense, the kingdom of God was breaking in, through the person of Christ. The long-awaited messianic rule, the beginning of God's restoration of the cosmos and of the hearts of His people, was beginning. Christ's death, burial, and resurrection signals Christ's victory over the cosmic powers, the defeat of sin, Satan, and death. And the entire New Testament pulsates with the news that the kingdom of God is here, as a living and expanding outpost of heaven, pointing forward to the Kingdom's full consummation when Christ returns.

This reality shatters, then, the kind of dualism we often see in the church and the world, where matters of faith and piety are restricted to Sunday worship inside the walls of the church. Christ's Kingdom reign has massive implications for how we think about our vocations, what we do with our work. If every square inch of the cosmos is under the lordship of Christ, our work is not a utilitarian exercise for The Man, but is a way we demonstrate, as God's Kingdom people, the restoration from brokenness that will be fully completed when Christ returns in victory at His Second Coming. Theologian John Frame writes:

> By his perfect life and spotless sacrifice, Jesus became a vicarious atonement for sin and undid the evil that the first Adam initiated. Moreover, the Second Adam is currently fulfilling the original mandate God had given to humanity.[47]

For the Christian, then, there is no divide between the distinctly sacred activities we do on Sundays and the "secular" things we accomplish on Mondays. This is why Paul says we do all things "to the glory of God" (1 Cor. 10:31; Col. 3:17), because Christ is "before all things, and by him all things hold together" (Col. 1:17). Your job on Monday is not a means to an end—it is part of your divine calling to fulfill the mandate given to us as God's image-bearers. The cubicle, the garage, the classroom—these are sanctuaries where you are called to worship your Creator with your best work.

We Are Not Heavenly-Minded Enough

"Absolute futility," writes the cynical poet of Ecclesiastes. "What does a person gain for all his efforts that he labors at under the sun? A generation goes, and a generation comes, but the earth remains forever" (Eccl. 1:2–4).

Many people view work as if it has no eternal value. You get up, you slug through traffic, you crank out work for somebody else, collect a paycheck, and repeat this until you are old enough to retire and then eventually you die. Someone throws dirt over your coffin and nobody remembers you. Or so it seems to go.

Christians are typically not as cynical, but they still often subscribe to a theory that minimizes the importance of vocation. Mostly, this is due to a sense that everything we do with our hands is trivial and fleeting. Scriptures such as 2 Peter 3:10, which describes a violent destruction of the earth, are taken to mean that Monday-through-Friday labors are temporary at best. How often have you heard a well-meaning message on the importance of mission that went something like this: "Nothing in this world matters except spreading the gospel." Or "Only what's done for Christ will last." In these reckonings, "what's done for Christ" narrowly refers to foreign missions or church activities. Think of how often we are feted with testimonies of the successful executive who "gave up his worldly ambitions" to "serve Christ."

These kinds of dualistic messages—that church work is what lasts and vocational work is meaningless—are based on a faulty reading of Scripture. Do Peter's words in 2 Peter 3:10 imply that the earth will be completely destroyed at the coming of Christ? Or do they imply a refining, purifying fire of renewal? John Piper says it is likely the latter:

> I'm inclined to say that Peter's description of a fiery destruction of creation in verses 10 and 12 doesn't refer to an annihilation of creation, but rather to a catastrophic purging and supernatural transformation of creation as God reverses the curse and makes all things new."[48]

Most of us have grown up hearing that everything we do in this life is ultimately unimportant and immaterial, because it will one day be destroyed when God comes to judge the world and consummate His Kingdom. But is this true?

Scripture seems to teach something different. In Romans 8, Paul says that creation will not be destroyed, but "set free from the bondage to decay" (Rom. 8:21). Remember, this is the creation that God calls "good" in Genesis 1:31. The earth, the psalmist writes in Psalm 24, is "the LORD's." God is in the business, through Christ, of renewing His world, not destroying it. This is why our work matters and will reverberate into eternity, not end when we are placed in the grave. Russell Moore explains:

> If the kingdom is what Jesus announced it is, then what matters isn't just what we neatly classify as "spiritual" things. The natural world around us isn't just a temporary "environment," but part of our future inheritance in Christ. Our jobs—whether preaching the gospel or loading docks or picking avocados or writing legislation or herding goats—aren't accidental. Our lives now are shaping us and preparing us for a future rule, and that includes the honing of a conscience and a sense of wisdom and prudence and justice. God is teaching us, as he taught our Lord, to learn in little things how to be in charge of great things (Luke 2; Matt. 25:14–23). Our lives now are an internship for the eschaton.[49]

Our work on earth, when done for the glory of Christ, passes the test of fire (1 Cor. 3:12–13) and is mere preparation for our perfected vocations in eternity. This joyful view not only imbues our everyday existence with meaning, but serves, to unbelieving coworkers, as a signpost of another world, an invitation to know Jesus and enter into the Christian story.

Work Means Everything

While there are many who struggle to find meaning in their everyday work lives, there are others for whom their career is the sole source of satisfaction. Work and calling can become idolatry.

What is often the first question you are asked when you meet someone for the first time? What is the first question you ask?

"What do you do for a living?" Our work is intrinsically tied to our identity. It's who we are.

I'm a writer.

I'm a pastor.

I'm a plumber.

I'm a financial advisor.

I'm an artist.

Work is a good gift from a great God. It is intrinsically tied into our identity as His image-bearers. But like all other good gifts from God, we can take what He made for our pleasure and make it ultimate. We begin to pursue, as objects of worship, what He has given us or we begin to worship ourselves and reject worship of God (Rom. 1:24–25). This is a tricky temptation.

We often don't realize we've worshipped at the altar of our careers until we've looked up and seen all of the unnecessary sacrifices we've made to this faceless god. Marriages. Children. Friendships. Mental health. Life purpose.

There is a reason the Ten Commandments begin with "Do not have other gods besides me" (Exod. 20:3). It's not simply because God is jealous and can't abide other deities. It's because anything less than God, even the good gift of a career, makes for a lousy deity. As gifts, they help us flourish and obey God's cultural mandate. As gods, they leave a path of wreckage, hopelessness, and broken promises. As a god, our careers demand everything from us, but offer us, at best, fleeting benefits in return.

Our problem is not that we are too ambitious to apply our gifts and fulfill our callings. Ambition, rightly ordered, is a good thing (Eccl. 9:10; Col. 3:23). Our problem is not even that we find pleasure in our life's work.

Work becomes idolatry when we find our identity in our work. If you belong to God, if you are His child through the death and resurrection of Christ—your identity is in Him. You were created in God's image, not in the image of your career. Only God can offer you the identity and worth and status you seek. In his book *Playing God,* Andy Crouch reminds us of the difference between imaging God by obedience to Him and treating the created gifts as divine:

The question is whether we are *making* idols—invest-
ing created things with ultimate significance—or
whether we are *being* idols in the sense of Genesis
1:26, images and signs of the ultimate truth about
the world. Whether we are idol makers or icons.[50]

What are some signs that we've become idol makers or icons
with our work? Here are a few telltale signs:

Poor Work and Life Rhythms

In his book, *Spiritual Rhythm*, Mark Buchanan contends
with the myth of balance:

> Our age has its own cherished myths, and one of
> the most hypnotic is the myth of balance. I hear it
> everywhere, from old and young, city dwellers and
> country folk, carpenters and lawyers, students and
> homemakers. Everyone seeks balance. Everyone longs
> for that magical combining of rest and lay and work
> that, once found, will make life simple, elegant, easy;
> balanced. Where is the perfect middle, they ask, the
> right proportion of duty and freedom, church and
> job, neighbors and family, time for others and time
> for me?
>
> There is none. It is no more to be found than
> unicorns and perfect churches.

There are only seasons, seasons for everything,
and seasons are inherently unbalanced.

The watchword for seasons isn't balance. It's
rhythm.[51]

Buchanan is right. Balance is mythical. Rhythm is vital
for spiritual health. There is no one-size-fits-all template. Every
season of life, every individual calling is different. What does
matter, what is important, is the motivation of the heart. What
gets first priority in our lives? What occupies our thoughts? What
shapes our ethics?

Personally, this always seems to show up in rather practical
ways. Quite often it's my children and my wife who diagnose this
idolatry before I do. I become absorbed in my phone and ignore
those around me. I work longer hours at home than is necessary. Every conversation is tinged with worry about my work.
I start eating too much and exercising too little. I stop reading
Scripture. I cease praying.

We were not designed for the 24/7, nonstop work life we are
tempted to embrace. We were made for work, but also for rest.
For when we rest, when we Sabbath, when we lay down our tools
and commit ourselves to the protection of God, we are demon-
strating trust in God.

When we eschew rest, when we seek to control and to know
and to manipulate everyone and everything, we reject the authority of God and become our own gods. However, when we make

regular time for rest, we remind ourselves and those around us that we are not God. We can close our eyes and trust the world to the One who holds the world together (Col. 1:17).

Slippery Ethics

If you are a fan of politics as I am, you may have watched the darkly cynical show *House of Cards*, which features as its main characters, Frank and Claire Underwood, a Washington, DC, power couple known for doing whatever it takes to accumulate power. What's interesting about the show is the evolution of their ruthlessness. They want to be in the White House and hold the levers of power and are willing to do anything—including kill, defame, and cheat—to get there.

Nobody wakes up one day, looks in the mirror, and says, "I want to ruin the lives of people so I can be significant." What does happen, however, is a gradual slippage of ethics, a slippery slope where one compromise makes the next compromise a little easier.

Few of us will have the opportunity to compromise our way into the White House, but in our own sphere of influence and power, we are tempted, daily, to make power and advancement such an idol that we forget who we worship. This is why it is so important for us to marinate, often, in the central truths of Scripture that tell us who really holds ultimate authority. Paul reminds us in Romans 13 that God is the one who sets up and takes down. David writes in the Psalms that promotion ulti-mately comes from the Lord (Ps. 75:7). Godly ambition is good, but a ruthless striving is evil (2 Tim. 2:24).

Again, nobody wakes up one day and decides to be a tyrant. Christians who abuse power and leadership do so by gradually drifting away from worship of Christ as King. Slowly, pride and narcissism form hard crusts around the soul.

We prevent this, mostly, by engaging regularly in the spiri-tual disciplines of silence, meditation, prayer, and weekly wor-ship. Each day we require reminders of our need for repentance and of our need to extend forgiveness. The gospel is the cleansing agent for our ambitious hearts and the ruthless destroyer of lesser gods.

We Think of Ourselves Higher Than We Ought to Think

In the late 1960s, when my father became a plumber's apprentice, blue-collar work was considered a noble and worthy profession. Today, as the West embraces what many have called a "knowledge economy," it is often the creative or cerebral voca-tions that are considered more valuable. In fact, those who work in the service industry or in the trades often face a stigma, as if their vocation is a kind of "fallback" position for people who can't get into college.

Those of us who write and speak for a living are tempted to think of ourselves and our work in a way that devalues those who are gifted differently. But this is not only pride, it is fundamentally at odds with the inherent dignity of all kinds of work. Tim Keller addresses this issue:

> The current economic era has given us fresh impulses and new ways to stigmatize work such as farming and caring for children—jobs that supposedly are not "knowledge" jobs and therefore do not pay very well. But in Genesis we see God as a gardener, and in the New Testament we see him as a carpenter. No task is too small a vessel to hold the immense dignity of work given by God. Simple physical labor is God's work no less than the formulation of theological truth.[52]

How we view the various professions is a good test on where we find our identity. If you consider your work more important than the work of others, it could be that you are finding your identity in your status instead of your Savior. And if you are discouraged because you consider your job lowly or demeaning, you also might be guilty of finding worth in what you do instead of whom you serve.

Conclusion

As we close this chapter, it's helpful to remember that God's view of work contrasts with the views of work we often hear in our culture. We are tempted toward two equally damaging ideas: work as meaningless or work as ultimate. The gospel reminds us that work is neither. It is a good gift from a great God.

Discussion Questions

1. Which cultural lie are you most tempted toward: work as meaningless or work as ultimate?
2. How has the Fall frustrated and corrupted your own work environment?
3. How does knowing that the God of the universe is at work add dignity to your work?
4. What are some ways a fresh and biblical approach to work can help you combat cultural lies and motivate you toward honoring God with your daily labors?

ADDITIONAL READING

Every Good Endeavor: Connecting Your Work to God's Work by Timothy Keller

Work Matters: Connecting Sunday Worship to Monday Work by Tom Nelson

Business to the Glory of God: The Bible's Teaching on the Moral Goodness of Business by Wayne Grudem

Your Work Matters to God by Doug Sherman

Kingdom Calling: Vocational Stewardship for the Common Good by Amy L. Sherman

ACKNOWLEDGMENTS

TO THE MANY HANDS INSIDE AND OUTSIDE THE ERLC, WE thank you for your help and assistance on this book. The ERLC team provided joyful encouragement in the planning and execution of this series, and without them, it would never have gotten off the ground. We want to also personally thank Phillip Bethancourt who was a major visionary behind this project. We'd also like to thank Jennifer Lyell and Devin Maddox at B&H, our publisher, for their work in guiding us through this process.

ABOUT THE ERLC

THE ERLC IS DEDICATED TO ENGAGING THE CULTURE WITH the gospel of Jesus Christ and speaking to issues in the public square for the protection of religious liberty and human flourishing. Our vision can be summed up in three words: kingdom, culture, and mission. Since its inception, the ERLC has been defined around a holistic vision of the kingdom of God, leading the culture to change within the church itself and then as the church addresses the world. The ERLC has offices in Washington, D.C., and Nashville, Tennessee.

ABOUT THE CONTRIBUTORS

Bruce Ashford is provost and professor of Theology & Culture at Southeastern Baptist Theological Seminary. He is the coauthor of *One Nation Under God* and *Every Square Inch*.

Daniel Darling is the vice president of Communications for the Ethics and Religious Liberty Commission and the author of several books, including *Activist Faith* and *The Original Jesus*. He is a regular contributor to *Christianity Today*.

Greg Forster serves as the director of the Oikonomia Network at the Center for Transformational Churches, and is a visiting assistant professor of Faith and Culture at Trinity International University. He has a PhD with distinction in political philosophy from Yale University. He is the author of six books, most recently *Joy for the World: How Christianity Lost Its Cultural Influence and Can Begin Rebuilding It*, and the coeditor of three books.

Bethany L. Jenkins writes, edits, and speaks on faith and work with The Gospel Coalition, The King's College, and the Center for Faith & Work at Redeemer Presbyterian Church in New York City.

Tom Nelson earned a Masters of Theology degree from Dallas Theological Seminary and a Doctor of Ministry Degree from Trinity International University. He is the author of *Five Smooth Stones: Discovering the Path to Wholeness of Soul, Ekklesia: Rediscovering God's Design for the Church,* and *Work Matters: Connecting Sunday Worship to Monday Work.* Tom is the president of Made to Flourish, a pastors' network for the common good. He also serves on the boards of The Gospel Coalition and Trinity International University. Tom has two grown children and has been married to his wife, Liz, for over thirty years.

Benjamin T. Quinn is assistant professor of Theology and History of Ideas at Southeastern Baptist Theological Seminary/ The College at Southeastern. He is the coauthor of *Every Waking Hour.*

NOTES

1. Paraphrase of Wendell Berry.

2. Amy L. Sherman, *Kingdom Calling: Vocational Stewardship for the Common Good* (Downers Grove, IL: InterVarsity, 2011), 67.

3. The Gospel Coalition, "Theological Vision of Ministry," *Foundation Documents*, http://www.thegospelcoalition.org/about/foundation-documents/vision.

4. J. R. R. Tolkien, "On Fairy-Stories," in *Tales from the Perilous Realm* (New York: Houghton Mifflin Harcourt, 2008), 336.

5. See http://theoldguys.org/2013/05/01/jonathan-edwards-god-designed-to-restore-all-the-ruins-of-the-fall/.

6. Quoted in a sermon by Tim Keller at Redeemer Presbyterian Church.

7. Andy Crouch, *Culture Making* (Downers Grove, IL: InterVarsity, 2008), 122.

8. Tim Keller, The Gospel Coalition 2013 Conference; see http://blog.acton.org/archives/55225-tim-keller-on-how-the-bible-shapes-the-way-we-work.html.

9. Tim Keller and Katherine Leary Alsdorf, *Every Good Endeavor* (New York: Penguin Books, 2012), 55.

10. Kevin DeYoung, *Just Do Something: A Liberating Approach to Finding God's Will* (Chicago, IL: Moody Publishers, 2009), 102.

11. "The life of the church is not exhausted in the act of assembly. Even if the church is not assembled, it does live on as a church in the mutual service its members render to one another and in its common

mission to the world." Miroslav Volf, *After Our Likeness* (Grand Rapids, MI: W. B. Eerdmans, 1998), 137.

12. Abraham Kuyper in a lecture prepared for seminary students.

13. Daniel Strange, "Rooted and Grounded? The Legitimacy of Abraham Kuyper's Distinction between Church as Institute and Church as Organism, and Its Usefulness in Constructing an Evangelical Public Theology," in *Themelios*, Vol. 40, Issue 3 (December 2015).

14. Luther's "Exposition of Psalm 147," in *Luther's Works, Volume 14.*

15. *Luther's Larger Catechism: With Study Questions*, trans. F. Samuel Janzow (Concordia, 1978), 90.

16. Amy L. Sherman, *Kingdom Calling: Vocational Stewardship for the Common Good* (Downers Grove, IL: InterVarsity Press, 2011), 103–4.

17. The Gospel Coalition, "Theological Vision of Ministry," see https://www.thegospelcoalition.org/about/foundation-documents/vision/.

18. Kevin DeYoung develops this argument in chapter 9 of *Just Do Something: A Liberating Approach to Finding God's Will* (Chicago, IL: Moody Publishers, 2009), 100–101.

19. Abraham Kuyper, *Common Grace* 1.1 (1853; repr., Bellingham, WA: Lexham Press, 2016).

20. The Gospel Coalition, "Theological Vision of Ministry," see https://www.thegospelcoalition.org/about/foundation-documents/vision/.

21. Tim Keller elaborates on this in *Every Good Endeavor*, reprint edition (New York, NY: Penquin Books, 2014).

22. See http://spu.edu/depts/uc/response/new/2012-autumn/features/more-than-a-paycheck.asp.

23. Oliver O'Donovan, *Resurrection and Moral Order: An Outline for Evangelical Ethics* (Grand Rapids, MI: Eerdmans, 1994), 13.

24. John P. Dickson, "Gospel as News: From Aristophanes to the Apostle Paul," *New Testament Studies* 51 (2005), 212–30.

25. Ibid.

26. This definition is taken from an unpublished manuscript by Bruce Ashford and Heath Thomas, "What Is the Gospel?"

27. Cf., Benjamin T. Quinn and Walter R. Strickland II, *Every Waking Hour: An Introduction to Work and Vocation for Christians* (Bellingham, WA: Lexham Press, 2016). Also, influenced by Lester DeKoster's definition of "work" in his *Work: The Meaning of Your Life: A Christian Perspective* (Grand Rapids, MI: Acton Institute, 2010).

28. We define work as "what creatures do with creation." Cf. Quinn and Strickland, *Every Waking Hour.*

29. Abraham Kuyper, from his inaugural address at the dedication of the Free University. Found in James D. Bratt, *Abraham Kuyper: A Centennial Reader* (Grand Rapids, MI: Eerdmans, 1998), 488.

30. John Behr, *Becoming Human: Meditations on Christian Anthropology in Word and Image* (Yonkers, NY: St. Vladimir's Seminary Press, 2013), 49.

31. Ibid., 56–57. Emphasis added.

32. See Luke 12:35–48 for a helpful reminder of the importance of stewarding God's world wisely as faithful servants who are ready for the Master's return.

33. Alexander Schmemann, *For the Life of the World* (Crestwood, NY: St. Vladimir's Seminary Press, 1973), 14. Also, see the Acton Institute film entitled *For the Life of the World* for an excellent cinematic portrayal of this point, in addition to a prescriptive approach to culture from a Christian perspective.

34. See Viktor E. Frankl, *Man's Search for Meaning* (1959; repr., Boston, MA: Beacon Press, 2006).

35. See James Davison Hunter in *To Change the World: The Irony, Tragedy, and Possibility of Christianity in the Late Modern World* (New York, NY: Oxford University Press, 2010), 198–212.

36. Dorothy Sayers, "Why Work?" in Mark R. Schwehn and Dorothy C. Bass, eds., *Leading Lives that Matter: What We Should Do and Who We Should Be* (Grand Rapids, MI: Eerdmans, 2006), 195.

37. Bill Peel and Walt Larimore, *Workplace Grace* (Longview, TX: LeTourneau University Press, 2014), 19.

38. The Hebrew word *para* conveys both procreativity and productivity. In Deuteronomy chapter 28 "para" describes the blessing and cursing of the fruit of the womb, fruit of the ground and fruit of cattle. (See Deut. 28:4, 11, 17.)

39. Yet each day we do our work, we realize that the work we do now is not what it ought to be.

40. The Greek term *tektōn* (pronounced as "teck-tone"), from which we derive such words as "tectonic" and "architect," has been translated in English as "carpenter." Yet some scholars are discovering that *tektōn* includes a greater range of skills and projects than our current understanding of carpentry. Based on his extensive word study, Ken Campbell suggests "builder" as the better translation: In the context of first-century Israel, the tektōn was a general craftsman who worked with stone, wood, and sometimes metal in large and small building projects. See https://tifwe.org/jesus-career-before-his-ministry/.

41. Our teaching team at the church I have the privilege of serving did a series on economics entitled "Neighborly Love." The six-week sermon series is available on our website (Christcommunitykc.org).

42. *The Theology of Work Bible Commentary* is the very insightful and helpful result of the Theology of Work project that brought together outstanding evangelical scholars who developed a helpful commentary on human work in every book of the Bible. It is faithful to sound doctrine and is accessible to the pastor. *The Theology of Work Bible Commentary* is published by Hendrickson, Peabody, Massachusetts, 2014.

43. Tom Nelson, *Work Matters: Connecting Sunday Worship to Monday Work* (Wheaton, IL: Crossway, 2011), 24–25.

44. Timothy Keller, *Every Good Endeavor: Connecting Your Work to God's Work*, reprint edition (New York, NY: Penguin Books, 2014), 77.

45. Found in *Abraham Kuyper: A Centennial Reader*, ed. James D. Bratt (Grand Rapids, MI: Eerdmans, 1998), 488, emphasis added.

46. Hugh Whelchel, *How Then Should We Work?: Rediscovering the Biblical Doctrine of Work* (Bloomington, IN: WestBow Press, 2012), 8.

47. John Frame, "Is Natural Revelation Sufficient to Govern Culture?" *Frame-Poythress.org*, May 21, 2012, http://frame-poythress.org/is-natural-revelation-sufficient-to-govern-culture/.

48. John Piper, "What Sort of Persons Ought You to Be?" *Desiring God*, May 13, 1982, http://www.desiringgod.org/messages/what-sort-of-persons-ought-you-to-be.

49. "You Only Live Forever," *Russell Moore*, accessed March 12, 2016, http://www.russellmoore.com/2015/11/03/you-only-live-forever/.

50. Andy Crouch, *Playing God: Redeeming the Gift of Power* (Downers Grove, IL: InterVaristy, 2013), 97.

51. Mark Buchanan, *Spiritual Rhythm: Being with Jesus Every Season of Your Soul*, first printing edition (Grand Rapids, MI: Zondervan, 2010), 197.

52. Keller, *Every Good Endeavor*, 37.

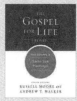

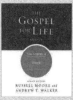